HOW TO START
AND MANAGE
A COUNSELING
BUSINESS

**CONTEMPORARY CHRISTIAN
COUNSELING**

HOW TO START AND MANAGE A COUNSELING BUSINESS

KATHIE ERWIN, Ph. D.

CONTEMPORARY CHRISTIAN COUNSELING

General Editor
GARY R. COLLINS, Ph.D.

HOW TO START AND MANAGE A COUNSELING BUSINESS
Contemporary Christian Counseling
Copyright © 1993 by Word, Incorporated

Library of Congress Cataloging-in-Publication Data:

Erwin, Kathie T., 1950–
 How to start and manage a counseling business/by Kathie T. Erwin.
  p. cm.—(Contemporary Christian Counseling)
 Includes bibliographical references and index.
 ISBN 0–8499–1085–4:
  1. Pastoral counseling—Practice. 2. Counseling—Practice. 3. Small business—Management. I. Title. II. Series.
 BV4012.2.E78 1993
 253.5′023—dc20   93–23348
                       CIP

3 4 5 6 7 8 9 LBM 7 6 5 4 3 2 1

Printed in the United States of America

In memory of my father,
Felix G. Tanner,
a talented sales and marketing executive

Contents

Acknowledgments

I am grateful to Dr. Gary Collins, General Editor, for the opportunity to be part of this excellent series. Having admired his books as a graduate student, I feel honored to work with him now as a colleague. My contacts at Word Publishing proved that they "practice what they publish" by providing technical assistance and encouragement in the true Christian spirit of fellowship. My thanks go to David Pigg, Manager of Academic and Professional Books, Project Editor Terri Gibbs, Copyeditor Sue Ann Jones, and Desktop Publishing Director Barry Kerrigan.

A key reason why this manuscript was completed on schedule was the input given by my husband, Dr. Bert Erwin. He challenged and questioned but never failed to leave drawings of smiling faces and affirming notes in the margins. He also took on additional responsibilities with our twin daughters, Robin and Kelly, while I worked on this book.

Let me also thank Clearwater Christian College and my alma maters, Liberty University and Eckerd College, for allowing me generous use of their academic libraries.

Chapter One

The Three-Rs of a Counseling Practice

It is not good to have zeal without knowledge, nor to be hasty and miss the way.

Proverbs 19:2

COUNSELING IS MORE THAN A MINISTRY, a calling, or a profession—counseling is also a business. Did your eyebrows rise at the notion that this honorable work might actually be something as commonplace as a business? Think again. There is nothing unholy about a successful business and nothing righteous about financially incompetent work. Balance is the key. Counseling ministries and private practices honor our Lord by operating on solid biblical and business principles.

At any beginning, Scripture reminds us to examine the motives of our hearts. You may be a pastor seeking the right way to add a counseling ministry in the church, or you may be a newly licensed professional counselor pondering whether to start your own practice or join a group of counselors. Maybe you have been working a few years in a social service agency and you feel your effectiveness is shackled by the secular environment. You may be a newcomer to counseling, a student, or a lay counselor searching for direction in your ministry. Any and all of these seekers can find the way toward more gratifying counseling ministries by examining and applying the business concepts presented in this book.

1

Let's start with the basics. Elementary school children learn the three Rs that represent reading, writing, and arithmetic. We need these, and, in addition, we need to understand the three Rs of a counseling practice: rationale, risks, and rewards.

Rationale

Why do you want your own counseling practice or ministry? Undoubtedly, you believe you have something unique to offer that is ordained by God—a common reason. A less noble sounding, yet often true, reason is the desire to work independently or to be in a position to direct the program. Yet we need to consider whether a counseling ministry will enhance a growing, evangelistic church. On the other hand, will such a ministry languish, unsupported, because the congregation does not share this vision? Are you called of God or fed up with calls from a demanding boss? In answering these questions, we must be totally honest about our motives.

Then there are other pertinent questions to consider when we want to establish the validity of our reasons for opening a counseling practice. For example:

What do you have to offer? Education, experience, specialized training, and the counselor's time comprise the *inventory* of a counseling center. Clients who come to counseling have a disadvantage in assessing the worth of your services. They can kick the tires at a used-car lot or squeeze the tomatoes at the grocery, but in selecting a counselor, they must make a quality judgment based on degrees, credentials, or titles that may or may not be a true reflection of clinical skills. States or provinces with counselor licensing laws regulate licensed professionals while other counselors continue to operate just outside of the legal parameters. To avoid client confusion and dissatisfaction, you need to present your qualifications clearly. Your client has a right to know whether your training is pastoral, professional, or paraprofessional and what level of expertise you have achieved.

Do you have any business experience? Counseling skills alone are not enough to sustain inept management. Good managers are good workers, but not all good workers make good managers. Someone must fill the complex role of counselor-administrator. Initially this role demands a daily mix of counseling, setting appointments, preparing reports, bookkeeping, and even making coffee. Whether you work in a one-person center or direct a full staff, you will have to understand and occasionally fill each role in the total operation.

Examine your work history for experience in managing resources or staff. Are you an innovative, inspiring leader, or are you more comfortable following a direction set by others? Do you see client problems and business setbacks as albatrosses or adventures? Management is similar to parenthood; both involve ongoing challenges, unexpected problems, adaptation to new stages, and the ability to render Solomon-like judgments with consistency and impartiality. Of course what you lack in experience you can bolster with study, internship, or mentorship in basic business administration, but ultimately there is no way to avoid the OJT (on-job-training) test to discover if you can implement what you have learned.

Are you an effective steward of your personal resources? The answer to this question could be found in how well you manage your personal finances. Does your use of money reflect an understanding of the difference between what you need and what you want? Or do you try to sneak wants in among the needs and beg God to supply the next payment on your boat or stereo system? That is pushing God and your budget over the limit. Scripture warns that "whoever can be trusted with very little can also be trusted with much, and whoever is dishonest with very little will also be dishonest with much" (Luke 16:10). In most instances, the financial habits that are nurtured at home will be repeated and magnified in business. That is why in order to be a successful business manager you must first prove yourself as a wise steward of personal resources.

RISKS

The only truly risk-free guarantee you get in this life is the security of salvation after accepting Christ as your personal Savior. Everything else is subject to risk. Financial planners are taught to identify their key investment risks (business, financial, interest rate, market, and purchasing power) and to be prepared to manage them. Likewise, counselors need to understand the risks inherent in a counseling business. It is much easier to develop appropriate strategies for dealing with risks that you know are likely to occur than to react in haste to risks that take you by surprise. Rather than deny or resist the risks that are involved in starting a counseling center, it is much wiser to identify the risks and deal with them rationally. Here are some of the universal risks inherent in a counseling ministry or private practice:

Financial. To give up a paycheck and wait for counseling fees or insurance reimbursements to arrive is a suspenseful waiting game very few can afford to play. Since a small or new counseling center is not likely to provide medical insurance, retirement plans, or other perks you may have enjoyed from your former agency or other employer, you need to consider whether you can afford to purchase these benefits out of your pocket. Without proper planning and budgeting of business expenses, you may not be able to keep your counseling center open long enough for it to become self-supporting.

Emotional. Believe me, the great relief you felt on the last day at your previous job will be offset by the burden you immediately shoulder in starting a new counseling practice, because the flip side of control is responsibility. You are now personally (and perhaps financially) responsible for the success or failure of this new business venture. And keep in mind that the time you will need to spend dealing with the daily frustrations of management will reduce the time you can spend counseling. For an inexperienced manager, the minor irritations can quickly magnify into major headaches. Then if you add the typical strain of business start-up to illness, family separation, or other losses, you have a perfect formula for disaster. Consider carefully: if this is a time of emotional instability for you and you are not able to handle pressure well, then it is probably not a good time to add the stress of new business developments.

Marriage and Family. How effectively you cope with the financial and emotional burdens of practice development will directly affect your spouse and children. In the initial months of preparing and launching your counseling center, your focus can become so limited that the ratio of work to family time becomes imbalanced. And when your spouse and children have to compete with the counseling center for your attention, you risk losing your primary calling of ministry in your own home. It is true, the expected (and unexpected) demands of a new business are a workaholic's dream. But that is why you need to decide if you can recognize the signs of work addiction and then delegate or moderate some of your duties to get your life back in balance.

Diminished reputation. Great ideas without great planning and administration can become grandiose failures. Too often the fast track to failure begins with overreaching management abilities, rejecting supervision and mentorship, or gambling that excessive expenditures will bring compensating returns. When you put your name and reputation behind a business, you and the business share a common fate. If your practice is unsuccessful and mismanaged, consider how that will affect your professional image and your potential for future employment in a managerial capacity.

What do you see as the risks to your counseling practice? Compare your answers with Dun and Bradstreet's survey of the causes of business failures shown in Table 1.1.

Table 1.1

Causes of Business Failures

Percent of Business Failures	Primary reasons for failure
64	Economic factors, insufficient profits, not competitive
24	Financial factors, business debts, excessive operating expenses, insufficient capital
7	Fraud by management or employees; disaster (fire, flood, burglary)
5	Neglect, lack of managerial experience, strategy mistakes, poor work habits, family problems, over-expansion

Source: Dun and Bradstreet Corp., Economic Analysis Department, 1992

Rewards

Financial Gain. If you can cope with the financial risks, you have the potential to enjoy financial rewards from your counseling practice. You can set your own fees and directly reap additional income from your labor and ideas. In a church-linked counseling ministry, your earnings may not be as high as in private practice; however, you have the eternal satisfaction of using your administrative skills to keep the ministry financially sound and providing service to the community.

Freedom. As a declared Christian counselor, you are free to practice your faith and your profession in one accord. You determine the client base, the types of counseling, and the hours of operation. Thus your work schedule may become more flexible and more productive with effective marketing and management.

Professional and Personal Satisfaction. Suddenly, going to work becomes a blessing, not a chore. You feel a sense of meaningful involvement in the counseling practice. If you work within a group practice, you may have an opportunity to pursue specialization in your area of greatest interest and skill. Each day as you see the Lord work in the lives of people through you and your colleagues, your own faith will be expanded.

Enhanced Reputation. Great ideas, along with great planning and accountability, often grow into great ministries! Your competence as a counselor-administrator can earn you respect from colleagues and clients. Other counselors, ministries, and professional organizations may call on you to share the ideas that built your successful counseling center. And this will provide additional ways to use your knowledge and business development experience to encourage other Christian counselors.

Are the potential rewards worth your time, effort and financial sacrifice? If you gain the independence and accolades, can you take pleasure in the achievement without losing focus?

When you understand the rationale, risks, and rewards of developing a counseling practice you will begin with an honest appraisal of your motives and expectations. You will be prepared to proceed through the planning process and action strategies to start or reorganize an effective counseling practice, which we discuss in the following chapters. As you take these methodical and, perhaps, unfamiliar steps, be mindful of the scriptural admonition that "an inheritance quickly gained at the beginning will not be blessed at the end" (Prov. 20:21). Let's not forget that opening a business in haste can provide ample opportunity to repent in leisure, unemployment, bankruptcy, or all of these dire possibilities. How much more profitable to invest a few weeks or months in careful preparation to launch a counseling center that will be a lighthouse to the hurting as well as a testimony to the unity of sound business and biblical principles.

Chapter Two

Developing Your Business Plan

Any enterprise is built by wise planning, becomes strong through common sense, and profits wonderfully by keeping abreast of the facts.

Proverbs 24:3–4 TLB

Do you remember the childhood party game Pin the Tail on the Donkey? Hitting the target with blindfolded eyes was nearly impossible. No matter how carefully you aimed, you never knew if you were successful until it was too late. The same is true of starting a counseling business without developing a business plan.

Counseling is a service that can minister to people of all ages and life situations. However, while that may be a description of humanity, it is not a realistic description of target clients. From that huge potential client base (humanity), you must describe the clients you seek and those who are most likely to use your services. Defining the target client is a means of blending *demographics* (a statistical view of population groups) and *services*. With the wealth of statistical data available from census, marketing, zoning, and university studies, it is fairly easy to zero in precisely on target populations. That is not to say that you want to draw a narrow description and ignore other potential clients who seek your services; yet, realistically, you will waste thousands of dollars in marketing if you fail to define your client demographics.

DEFINING YOUR TARGET CLIENT

Although your counseling center may be capable of serving several different populations, it is best to begin by defining the primary client for your services. First, determine an age group by carefully considering what that age group needs and how your services can meet those needs. Do you have skills to work with children and adolescents? Are you more comfortable counseling adults? Can you work with geriatric clients? Most centers accept both men and women. Will you specialize in gender-specific counseling? Posing questions like these will help you to focus on the group(s) of people you can best serve in your counseling center.

Another way to describe your target client is by lifestyle. This includes children living under the authority of others, college students, adult singles, married couples, and elder adults living alone or in assisted care. Lifestyle also applies to some choices that fall outside of biblical traditions, such as unmarried couples living together, gays and lesbians, and people living in abusive relationships. Do any of these lifestyles typify your target client? Do any of these potential clients represent a population that cannot be helped in your center, either because of limited professional skills or personal preference? Are you willing to work with clients in non-biblical relationships who do not seek a lifestyle change? If there are any groups that you cannot work with due to lack of expertise or preference, be prepared to refer them to another competent counselor. You don't have to work with every type of client who enters your door. However, as a Christian and as a professional, you need to make an appropriate referral and encourage those persons to pursue counseling elsewhere.

Income is an important demographic element of lifestyle that must be considered because your income potential from counseling is directly related to the income level of your target client. Now some socioeconomic aspects of lifestyle are more apparent than others. For example, a majority of retired elder adults depend on a fixed income that may be severely pinched during times of high inflation. In other groups, income levels vary dramatically. Adult singles range from struggling single parents to young designer-clad executives. Without assuming any stereotypes, gather solid financial information on your potential clients. Income statistics within your area are readily available from your public library, local newspaper marketing department, city or county planning and zoning board, or local college and university libraries. Write a short letter detailing the specific demographic data you seek and request an appointment to discuss this information. You can expect to find that many statisticians and librarians are artisans at matching marketing problems with demographic profiles.

The location of your office is the next factor in formulating your client description. To make this process easier, get a city map. Using a compass with the point set on your proposed office location, draw a circle roughly equivalent to a five-mile radius. This is your primary service area. Then draw a second circle equal to a ten-mile radius. This is your secondary service area.

Study the population within your primary service area. What are the demographic characteristics in terms of age, sex, ethnic background, lifestyle, income, mobility, marital status, and religious affiliation? These things will tell you volumes about the client potential within your office location. With this information you can determine whether your counseling practice and your neighborhood are compatible. You can't run an inner-city counseling ministry from a suburban church office. Nor can you consistently attract busy families if you are located far from family-oriented housing. If a significant proportion of your target clients are lower income and lack personal transportation, check on the availability of public transportation. Know the location of bus stops or subway stations near your office. Without public transportation, your client base may be limited to people who live within walking distance and those who have a car.

Gaining clients from the secondary service area is slightly more challenging as the distance increases. Because regardless of the increased mobility of modern society, we still suffer from a convenience store mentality. You can be sure that your clients will drive across town for dinner at a chic restaurant much more readily than they will drive the same distance for counseling. That is why in many larger cities, counselors offer several types of therapy from a variety of religious and nonreligious foundations. Even in smaller communities, counseling offices are likely to be scattered in several different areas. Due to the time pressures of work and family, clients tend to choose a counselor whose office is close to their home or workplace. So make sure you know whether your target clients live within your primary service area.

Next, take a bright-colored pen and place a dot at the location of every counseling center, psychologist, private-practice counselor, and church that offers counseling to the public. These are alternative service providers within your primary and secondary service areas. (Note the word *competition* was carefully reframed to *alternative service provider*. Nevertheless, you may find your center in direct competition with other providers, both Christian and secular.) You will have a better perspective of how your proposed services could overlap with existing services if you research the demographics and counseling programs of other nearby providers.

TYPES OF SERVICES

What makes your service stand out? One possible answer is theology. But you cannot simply tack *Christian* on to your center's nameplate and assume everyone knows what you mean. You need to prepare a brief statement of your faith that will tell your clients where you stand on theological issues. Then you have other decisions to make regarding your clients' spiritual affiliations. Do you want to work only with members of your own denomination? Can you work comfortably with any client who believes in the whole Bible as God's truth? What about clients who call themselves Christian but have a theological system that is vastly different from yours? If your center is located separately from a church and offers reasonable fees, you will probably attract many non-Christians and unchurched Christians.

At the same time you must be watchful to accept only those clients you have the proper training and ability to counsel. Good theology is not a substitute for competent counseling. Regrettably, much unskilled, damaging counseling is done in the name of the Lord. A better approach is described in the title of Larry Crabb's book, *Effective Biblical Counseling*. Work so that you are equally effective in displaying your biblical foundations and your counseling expertise.

After identifying your target client by demographics, determine the type of services that can be provided in your counseling center. Are you best qualified by training and supervised experience to counsel with individuals, groups, or families? Individual counseling is the most common practice, with sessions ranging from forty-five to sixty minutes. Yet even the concept of "individual" counseling is too broad. Without a clear definition of your counseling specialties, individual counseling presents a smorgasbord of human problems that can stretch your skills to the breaking point. Some state licensing laws set limits for counselors as to the types of counseling they can practice (i.e., psychotherapy, sex therapy, substance-abuse treatment) as well as the qualifications that are necessary to diagnose, evaluate, and treat problems of a psychological nature.

Group counseling is a productive use of the therapist's time and a cost-effective means of providing care to clients who could not afford individual session fees. However, we need to keep in mind a word of caution: Group therapy is more than *doing group*. Geese flock, churches congregate, adolescents hang out, but therapeutic group counseling demands more than gathering several individuals to chat and trade memories. Whether you seek to conduct a therapy group, a growth group, or a support group, first make sure you have the proper training to fully understand group processes. Become familiar with the code of ethics of the Association for Specialists in Group Work (ASGW)[1] or use other professional ethical standards to guide your work as a group counselor or co-facilitator.

Family counseling combines some techniques of individual and group counseling and applies them to a set of clients with problematic family relationships. The lines between family therapy and pastoral counseling of families can easily blur.

How clearly are these types of counseling (therapeutic and pastoral) delineated in your practice or church-linked counseling center? Do you have the qualifications to recognize and facilitate family counseling that deals with violation of boundaries, abuse, overcontrol or undercontrol, multigenerational and multicultural struggles, or family system response to a psychopathological member? If not, decide what types of family counseling you can responsibly and legally provide.

Another type of counseling service involves tests and assessments. These range from personality profiles to career-interest inventories to diagnostic instruments. With appropriate credentials, you can incorporate testing into your counseling service or offer it as a specialty. (Various ways of blending testing services into a marketing strategy will be presented later in chapter 8.) But remember, you cannot ethically use any test or assessment unless you meet the educational, experience, and/or license qualifications stated in the test manual or catalog.

Along this same line of service are career counseling and guidance, which have grown beyond the high school and college campus. As more adults change jobs several times during their working years (by choice or otherwise), career counseling is gaining wider acceptance. This can become a feature attraction in your counseling center if you have the ability to utilize appropriate testing and assessment instruments, can network with educational and community resources, and can guide your clients through the emotional aspects of career change.

Your Mission Statement

First, your mission statement represents the purpose and philosophy of your business. Think of it as the one-minute theme of what you do, who you serve, and what beliefs guide your practice. Even the apostles worked from a mission statement given by Jesus:

> Therefore go and make disciples of all nations, baptizing them in the name of the Father and of the Son and of the Holy Spirit, and teaching them to obey

everything I have commanded you. And surely I am with you always, to the very end of the age. (Matt. 1:19–20)

Look at how the Great Commission meets all the elements of an effective mission statement: what you do—disciple, baptize, teach; who you serve—all nations; what belief guides your practice—to work in the name of the Father, the Son, and the Holy Spirit by following the commands of Jesus. Two thousand years later, this mission statement still motivates Christians.

From that context we derive the title *missionary* as a person who attempts to convert others to a way of life, belief, or action. The *mission* of any business is to generate interest in specific products or services, and to motivate a client to believe he or she will benefit from the products or services and, thus, will act on that belief by seeking what is offered. If there is no need or demand for your counseling center, it serves no purpose and, therefore, will not continue as a viable business operation.

Second, devise a mission statement that is action oriented and goal driven. State your mission in concise, expressive language that can be read verbally in one minute. Here are two contemporary examples:

> 1. Christian Counseling Center provides counseling for families experiencing stress, communication breakdown, or discipline problems. Our goal is to strengthen families of All American City by offering Christ-centered counseling and parenting groups, on a sliding scale, to make counseling affordable to everyone. Christian Counseling Center is a nonprofit service sponsored by First Church of All American City.

> 2. Able and Baker Counseling Associates are licensed counselors specializing in individual and group counseling for eating disorders, anorexia, bulimia, depression, and self-image issues. Our services blend professional psychotherapy and biblical

Christianity. Through our three Urban County offices and our affiliate program at Wellness Hospital, ABC seeks to raise awareness of eating disorders, provide effective treatment, and offer relapse-prevention support groups in our community.

Finally, the mission statement keeps your focus on the task. My pastor, Dr. Charlie Martin, continually reminds our congregation that "the main thing is to keep the Main Thing the main thing." This simple prompting brings us back from those pleasant sidetracks (dinners, meetings, and social activities) to the Main Thing (the Great Commission). Allow your mission statement to be your compass; use it regularly to check your direction. It will be the answer to those persistent questions, "And what do you do?" or "What is so great about this counseling center?" It will also be a key in promoting your business—why not print your mission statement on the back of your business card (see why it needs to be compact!). When you know what your main thing is, it will be easy to tell if you are remaining on course toward the Main Thing.

Now, it is your turn. Describe the significant aspects of your counseling center in one or two short paragraphs that can be read in less than one minute. Ask several people of various ages (not other counselors) to read the description and restate it in their own words. If they can do this, you have probably drafted an effective, understandable mission statement. If they can't, then you need to review and simplify your statement.

YOUR BUSINESS PLAN

If you typically resist preparing an outline for term papers, sermons, or seminars, go ahead and grump before reading any farther. The most productive and (for some of you) painful part of the start-up process is writing the business plan. "But isn't defining my target client and writing a mission statement enough?" protest those who are organizationally disadvantaged. Unfortunately, no. "Dreaming instead of doing is foolishness" (Eccles. 5:7 TLB). So why not put your dreams of service into a workable form? The information that you have gathered and the decisions you have made up to this point can serve as the building blocks of your business plan.

An appropriate beginning for a business plan is the mission statement. In addition, the plan also consists of:

Management Summary. This explains the chain of command and states the specific responsibilities of each person who has authority over other counselors or staff. Remember to include a copy of your organizational flow chart. Even in a small organization, a chart indicating lines of direct authority and responsibility are important for smooth day-to-day operations.

Counseling Staff Summary. Here is the place to present mini-biographies of the counselors who provide direct client services. Emphasize education, professional qualifications or licensure, and experience that relates to each counselor's ability to offer high-quality client service. Include a brief statement from each counselor that portrays his or her therapeutic approach.

Demographic Review. Begin with a narrative description of the characteristics of those your counseling center seeks to serve. Also include a map with the circles encompassing your primary and secondary service areas. Any charts that will enhance the narrative are a great way to add visual impact and to draw the reader's attention to your demographic picture. In order to add credibility to this review, be sure to note the demographic sources used (i.e., census figures, county planning surveys, etc.).

Target Client. Give an explanation of the population you serve as described by age, sex, ethnic background, lifestyle, income, location, and theology. If you have more than one target client group, give the characteristics of each group. You may also want to compare and contrast the differences in the two target groups either in narrative form or with a chart. With two or more target groups a colorful pie chart is a simple way to show what percentage each group is expected to represent among your total client base.

Type of Services. Be specific in describing your services and avoid jargon or professional terms that would confuse those who are unfamiliar with counseling. For example, state that you work with "engaged or married couples," not "dyads." On the other hand, you don't want to go overboard with abstract generalities—"counseling for children" is too general and easy to misinterpret. Instead, specify "we counsel children ages seven through twelve."

It is also a good idea to demonstrate with brief examples how your services meet the needs of the target clients in your primary and secondary service areas. Let the reader know why your services are innovative, highly qualified, and capable of fulfilling unmet needs in the primary and secondary target areas.

Marketing Strategies. You need to determine how you will reach your target client, at what cost, and with what measure of effectiveness. A good foundation for these marketing strategies is the demographic and service sections you have already completed. Remember that a strategy is a plan of action, it is not a to-do list. In other words, "write and print brochures" is for a to-do list; "we have made arrangements to distribute brochures at the county-wide ministerial association to increase awareness of our services among multi-denominational pastors" is a strategy. If you present a detailed marketing budget to support your strategies, be certain that the total expenses or projected expenses also appear in appropriate areas of the section on financial status and projections. By making a breakdown of marketing expenses that relate to the proposed strategies you indicate that you have a plan and have calculated how much funding is required to support it.

Financial Status and Projections. This category includes statements of where you are (your balance sheet) and where you aspire to be (cash-flow projections) with the balance of significant information being presented in the numbers rather than the narrative. Other information that will be necessary includes a projected cash budget for start-up, an anticipated cash budget for monthly operations, and a projected income statement. It can be extremely helpful to ask an accountant to review this data for proper format and to verify accuracy. Regardless of the size of your business, comprehensive financial statements are a necessary element of a business plan. For a new business, comprehensive forms may have fewer columns and categories than a larger company's statements, but they still present a detailed view of the operation's true financial status.

Thus, within the business plan, a complete picture emerges of the framework in which your counseling center will exist. It includes macroenvironmental data describing general economic health, the demographics of your target client compared with the general population, social trends, and the applicable laws regulating counseling. Microenvironmental data are also included in your business plan. They reflect conditions in your primary and secondary service areas such as demand for counseling services, competition, and the availability of community mental health agencies.[2]

Before you are ready to formally present your business plan, talk it over with your church board and your associate counselors. Or, if you are starting a solo practice, ask several trusted Christian business managers to be your sounding board. This exercise will identify inconsistencies and inadequacies in the plan or will affirm its merit. Seek as much competent input as possible. When you are personally involved in a project like this, it is easy to overlook or overestimate strategic factors. But by talking with other counselor-administrators, church administrators, private-practice healthcare providers, and local business owners you can gain a more objective perspective through the benefits of their experiential insight.

Another good reason to prepare and update a business plan is that banks or private lenders will request it if you need to ask them for a start-up or expansion loan. Many lenders have a list of information that is required in such planning, however, format is not as critical as content. Much like an architect's blueprint, a business plan needs to display clearly the materials, the building stages, and the completed view.

A business plan is also important for counselors and ministers who are making a proposal for the addition of a counseling center to the local church, or for those who are seeking sponsorship for a church-linked counseling center. In this process, the governing board (deacons or elders) represents the lender (the church) who makes a decision, based on information presented in the plan, whether to financially support a counseling center. And counseling ministries that operate as nonprofit corporations need a sound business plan just as much as profit-oriented businesses do. It goes without saying that financial accountability and careful planning are necessary elements of good stewardship for all counselors.

When you prepare your business plan keep in mind that they tend to be a lot like term papers. Some (prepared by devoted obsessives) are the size of the Los Angeles telephone directory—they drown the reader in statistics and charts—while others are extra-wide-margin attempts to make puny information stretch over a task half-done. Both of these approaches get failing grades. Aim for a happy medium—give enough information to address each key topic but don't go on a chart binge. A successful business plan is not measured in pages, but in substance. Consider the ten most common mistakes made by novices in preparing a business plan.

1. Inadequate demographic research.
2. Target market too broad or poorly defined.
3. Target market too narrow to support an additional competitor.
4. Start-up costs underestimated.
5. Marketing and advertising budget too small to fund grandiose plans.
6. Failure to survey the competition.
7. First-year income overestimated.
8. Inadequate or inaccurate financial statements and projections.
9. Unrealistic projections of income relative to the local market.
10. Failure to convey an impression of how this business is different from the competition and why it is needed in the local market.

Too often would-be entrepreneurs decide not to take the time to prepare a business plan and jump right into doing business. Please resist that temptation! If you can't make your business work on paper, you probably won't be able to make it work in reality. Major corporations know this. They use simulations to try out new products and to project their adaptability in various economic situations. Preparing a business plan is a less expensive form of simulating operations for the start-up year and setting goals for future years. And the advantage is that the mistakes you make on paper can be erased and improved without any adverse affects on your working capital! In contrast, the mistakes you make in operation can wipe out your business—permanently.

The final step in this process is the most challenging—putting the business plan into action. You have invested too much labor into this project to allow it to become another dust-catcher on your bookcase. Keep a working copy of your plan near your desk or in your tickler file. It will be the road map for where your business is heading and the yardstick for measuring progress. An effective business plan becomes frayed and worn from frequent use during the start-up year. But remember, it is not written in stone. With experience, you may discover that certain elements need to be revised and the budget figures adjusted accordingly. That is fine as long as you are revising within the plan and not project hopping or moving into new areas without adequate study. You might say a business plan is a fluid document with a solid foundation. It may change; yet it never strays too far from its base. And the operations must always complement the mission statement.

After the first year, you will have a reasonable perspective of the flow of clients, of busy versus slow seasons, and of the real cost of operations. There's nothing like experience and actual numbers to help you revise your business plan for the second year and to set new or expanded goals. In fact, even after the start-up year its a good idea to read your plan quarterly or at least semiannually. You may only scan it briefly, without making an analytical review, but even this will reinforce your goals, recall marketing ideas, and renew your commitment to service.

NOTES

1. *Ethical Guidelines for Group Counselors*, as approved by the Executive Board of the Association for Specialists in Group Work, 1 June 1989. ASGW is a

division of the American Association for Counseling and Development, Alexandria, Virginia.

2. William J. Winston, *How to Write a Marketing Plan for Health Care Organizations* (New York: Haworth Press, 1985).

Chapter Three

Structuring Your Counseling Practice

Unless the LORD *builds the house, its builders labor in vain.*

Psalm 127:1

BUILDING A HOME IS AN OPPORTUNITY to display your personal style. The exterior of your home may be modern, classic with columns, or Victorian; it may even look like a log cabin. Regardless of the image projected by each exterior, the family and personal lifestyles conducted inside those walls can be the same as those conducted in any dwelling. Similarly, in determining the structure of your business, you will still practice counseling according to your skills and interests, no matter which type of organizational form you choose. The different methods of organization presented in this chapter relate to business and tax issues.

Like other business people, counselors must choose the structure, that is the legal and operational framework, within which their business will develop. The tax status and certain operational features are closely related to the formal or informal nature of that business structure. For instance, a partnership or a corporation that is designated as a professional association is a formal structure that requires specific legal and tax treatments. In contrast, a sole proprietorship or a counselor working in a nonemployee relationship with another counselor constitutes an informal structure. Another option, the nonprofit church-linked counseling ministry, is discussed in chapter 4. Since the objective of this chapter is to make business structure understandable for counselors with limited entrepreneurial experience, we have chosen to use as little technical jargon as possible. And do remember that what you read here is not a substitute for professional legal or tax advice. Rather, the intention is to motivate you to seek professional advice on any matters that are out of your range of knowledge.

FORMAL STRUCTURE: PARTNERSHIP

A business partnership is a legal relationship between two or more individuals who choose to be co-owners; each contributes money, property, labor, or skill and expects to share in the profits or losses.[1] The typical partnership begins with two individuals. Like a good marriage, a successful business partnership necessitates the commitment of both parties to the same goals, to a shared workload, and to mutual respect. Such a commitment is solidified in a partnership agreement that serves as the governing document of the business relationship.

PARTNERSHIP AGREEMENT

The partnership agreement specifies how the partners will initiate, operate, expand, and dissolve the business. This is where all the "what if?" questions are addressed. What happens if the partners disagree on a major expenditure? How are profits and losses divided? What if one partner contributes more start-up cash than the other partner? What happens to the business if one partner retires, becomes disabled, or dies? These are only samples of the important questions that need to be answered within a partnership agreement that is drafted by one attorney or in a joint effort by attorneys representing each prospective partner.

Determining beforehand who will be responsible for what jobs will dramatically reduce the stress of daily decisions. For example, you may decide that the partner with business experience will function as the counselor-administrator, dealing with staff and other business decisions, while the other partner will concentrate on case management and developing new managed-care contracts. This is a logical division of labor based on skills. In order to clarify such business roles, the partners need to write their own job descriptions based on the division of authority that is described in the partnership agreement. Thus, rather than creating a partnership and continuing to work separately, the two counselors combine their skills for maximized potential.

Who Contributes What

In years past, it was traditional for the bride to bring a dowry of property or other assets into a marriage to finalize the commitment. Things are more egalitarian in business partnerships. Generally, each business partner is required to make some mutually agreeable contribution before the commitment is signed. Thus begins a delicate balancing act based on who contributes what. As a counselor, you know the difficulties that exist when one spouse feels he or she has invested more in the marriage than the other. It is no different in business. Each partner must feel that his or her contribution of assets or skills is appropriately valued and expectations of profit are fairly distributed. For both legal and tax purposes, accurate values of any property (i.e. furniture, computer, copier) brought into the partnership must be recorded. This is known as the *basis* or amount of investment in the property for tax purposes and is not a matter to be treated casually. Determining the basis of assets can mean the difference between money saved or more tax dollars owed. Consult with your accountant on the correct methods to record the cost basis (actual price) or adjusted basis (increased or decreased by certain events). Also, consider this word of caution from the IRS: "You must know the basis of your interest in the partnership to figure your allowable deduction for partnership losses [or to] dispose of your interest in the partnership."[2] Very simply, if partners do not agree on the value of what the partnership owns, they will have problems agreeing on the fair division of those assets. That is why attorneys who deal with business agreements are accustomed to wearing a Solomon hat when helping partners divide and balance assets with other contributions.

Still other complications can arise over compensation for differing workloads. As any counselor knows, counseling is not a nine-to-five business. Clients fail to keep appointments and crisis calls create unexpected overtime work. In fact, accepting an unpredictable schedule is part of the counselor's job. However, what happens if one partner works fewer income-generating hours than the other partner yet he or she wants to share equally in the profits? Likewise, can one partner continue to participate equally in profits or losses while on vacation or sick leave? These problems of equal pay for unequal work need to be clarified in the partnership agreement. Partnerships are destroyed more thoroughly by resentment than by financial losses.

ADVANTAGES AND DISADVANTAGES OF PARTNERSHIPS

One advantage of working in a formal partnership is that it is a well-defined operational system that is formal in appearance but has fewer reporting requirements than a corporation has.

Another advantage is that under the terms of the partnership agreement, profits and losses pass to individual partners, which are then taxed at the individual rate. Furthermore, arrangements can be made to protect the financial interest of a partner's surviving spouse and family.

Among the disadvantages of a partnership is unlimited liability. The poor decisions or misdeeds of one partner, who acts in the name and authority of the partnership, can create economic and personal hardship on all the partners. In fact, disagreement can be as paralyzing as mistakes in that a two-person partnership may be stalemated if both partners fail to agree on a course of action. In addition, if the business is faltering, all partners may be required to make mandatory contributions to remain in operation. For the hardworking but cash-deficient partner who has already put all his or her available assets into the business, this may mean giving up a percentage of ownership to the cash-rich partner who makes up the financial deficit. If one partner withdraws from the business or dies, a forced dissolution of the partnership may occur if the other partner is unable or unwilling to purchase the abandoned partnership interest.

Talk with your accountant and attorney about how these and other aspects of a partnership apply in your situation. Above all, don't think you will save money or headaches by avoiding these legal issues during an unofficial trial partnership before meeting with an attorney. Co-habitating without the benefit of a legal partnership agreement is as financially foolish in business as it is in personal relationships.

The Buy-Sell Agreement

Many factors limit the longevity of a partnership. At any time, one partner may be compelled to withdraw due to disability, bankruptcy, divorce, loss of professional license, or death. If that happens, partners may agree to disagree, concluding that their personalities and workstyles are incompatible. Or the elder partner may want to prepare for a smooth transition at retirement by taking steps to provide retirement income from his or her share of the business. Situations like these are provided for well in advance of the occurrence with a *buy-sell agreement*. This is a complex, legally binding agreement that needs to be drawn up by an attorney in consultation with your accountant and financial planner.

A buy-sell agreement provides for the orderly transfer of a partner's interest under any of the situations previously described. It also answers more "what if?" questions. For example, upon the death of a partner, how rapidly will the interests be liquidated? What happens to the deceased partner's share of partnership debt? As a way to protect estate interests, can the surviving spouse assume the deceased partner's management role during the buy-out period? After the death of a partner and before the settlement is complete, are the deceased partner's spouse or heirs entitled to continue receiving a share of the partnership income? Will there be provisions for a disability buy-out if a partner is totally disabled? These important questions seem remote in the initial stages of forming a new business, yet such settlement issues all too frequently generate legal battles that can rapidly strangle the assets of a small business, leaving behind only bitterness and bankruptcy.

Neither a new business nor one that is expanding is likely to have enough cash to handle a buy-out. Thus, the most common method of funding a buy-sell agreement is with life insurance. The cost of premiums to purchase sufficient life insurance to cover each partner's share of the buy-out is relatively inexpensive depending on the ages and health of the partners. A life insurance agent who has experience in working with buy-sell agreements is a good source for this pertinent information. (Some insurance companies offer special plans for business use.) It is also a good idea to inquire about coverage for a disability buy-out in the event of the partial or complete disability of a partner.

Another way to avoid legal problems is to have each partner's spouse sign the buy-sell agreement at the time it is formally executed. In this way, the spouse knows how much or how little reliance to place on obtaining a share of the business in the event of death or divorce.

PROFESSIONAL ASSOCIATION OR PROFESSIONAL CORPORATION

Being part of a professional association or professional corporation adds an impression that yours is an important business. By incorporating, your fledgling counseling business shares a similar legal structure with the major *Fortune 500* companies. Unfortunately, what many people misunderstand is that a business does not have to be big to be a corporation. In fact, in the United States, closely-held (sole or few owners) and family-held corporations greatly outnumber large corporations—the ones that own the places where you shop, eat, and get your car repaired.

Although you and your closely-held corporation may seem like one and the same, for tax and legal purposes your corporation is a separate entity with an identity and life of its own. So dramatic is this separation that a corporation is sometimes referred to as an *artificial person*; it has a business life that can continue longer than your life on earth. The extent of your control in the corporation depends on the number of shares of stock you own. In a closely-held corporation you may be the only shareholder. In other situations the percentage of stock ownership may be split according to predetermined factors such as the amount of investment in the company.

An increasing number of new counseling businesses are choosing to incorporate because the PA (professional association) or PC (professional corporation) after the business name gives the appearance of professionalism that is commonly used in the medical community. Another reason for the popularity of incorporating is that the shareholder's liability for corporate debt is limited to the amount of his or her investment in the corporation. But there is a word of caution in this regard: If you are both a corporate shareholder and a provider of services, you are not totally insulated from the loss of personal assets. For example, a disgruntled client may sue both the corporation and you, individually, as the service provider. You cannot count on a corporation to shield you or limit your losses in a professional liability situation.

The PA and PC are the typical corporation structures used by counselors and other mental health professionals. Whether your business can incorporate as a professional association or professional corporation depends on the laws in your state. Since many physicians, dentists, and other medical providers operate as a PA or a PC, clients are accustomed to seeing this business structure in conjunction with the healthcare community. Besides PA and PC, other common terms that refer to different types of corporations are C, S, and nonprofit. C and S status relate to tax issues, which are discussed in chapter 9, and nonprofit corporations are discussed in chapter 4.

Articles of Incorporation

Your corporation is born as soon as the articles of incorporation are filed with the appropriate agency of the state in which the corporation is registered. These articles can be simple or complex, depending on the scope of corporate operations; but for most counseling practices the articles of incorporation are simple and concise. The primary information they contain is the official name of the corporation, the date of the opening of the business, the proposed term of its existence, its purpose, the name and address of the registered agent, the names of the board of directors, and the amount, class, and value of corporate stock. In defining the purpose of the corporation, be careful not to paint yourself into a corner. A center that limits its initial activities to counseling for family issues may later want to expand its services to include the sale of educational materials or training programs for family counselors. So it makes sense to define the purpose of the corporation in terms that easily permit expansion. In some states the article that declares the purpose can be written to allow transaction of any and all lawful business that is permitted under your state corporation laws. This question of defining the purpose of your business as well as the decision on what types and amount of stock to issue are matters that need to be discussed carefully with your attorney while the articles are being drafted.

After the articles have been recorded by the applicable state agency, you will receive a letter indicating the document number of your corporation and the recording date, which is important because it is the official starting date of your corporation. In our family-owned businesses, we always pay the small extra fee to get a certified copy of the articles of incorporation. This certified copy is sealed by the state and presents an impressive official image. There also may be occasions, such as financial transactions or legal actions, when a certified copy is required.

BYLAWS

If you have any prior experience with clubs or civic associations, you are no doubt aware that these organizations function under rules known as bylaws. So, too, does your corporation. The bylaws of your corporation give the details of important provisions for operating your business, including rules for shareholders' meetings, the definition of a quorum to conduct business meetings, functions of the board of directors, election and removal of corporate officers, how to issue or transfer corporate stock, how to conduct business meetings, and provisions for amending these rules. Much of the language and sections of the bylaws are already in your attorney's computer and can be customized as needed. Some attorneys and business owners purchase corporate kits for recordkeeping that contain fill-in-the-blank bylaws. Whether your document is custom tailored or off-the-rack, read it carefully and seek legal advice for any sections that you do not fully understand or know how to implement.

CORPORATE MINUTES

If the corporation's articles of incorporation represent its birth certificate, and the bylaws represent its etiquette guide, then the minutes represent its personal diary. Minutes are a record of the actions taken by the shareholders, including election of officers and directors. Another set of minutes records the meetings of the board of directors. If all of this sounds a bit excessive for a fledgling counseling practice, be assured that there are ways to meet these demands on a smaller scale. For instance, if your state incorporation laws permit, you can be the sole subscriber and sole director of your own corporation. In the one-person corporation, it may seem peculiar to hold a meeting with yourself, yet the annual meeting requirement still needs to be fulfilled.

The most important aspect of corporate minutes is that they must be complete and up to date. Accurate recording of actions taken by the directors or shareholders can serve as important substantiation for issues such as employee benefits, designation of an officer to sign contracts or make investments on behalf of the corporation, authorization of capital (major) expenses, and decisions regarding salaries, bonuses, or dividends. All significant actions that involve corporate assets, create debts, bind the corporation to provide services, alter leadership, or otherwise affect corporate operations in a way that requires approval from the board of directors or shareholders must be recorded in the minutes. Failure to document these actions can result in costly tax and legal complications. If you are concerned about format, ask your attorney for a sample copy of corporate minutes. Or look at sample minutes in books on corporate forms and corporate organization; these books are available inexpensively at office supply stores and at the public library.

ADVANTAGES AND DISADVANTAGES OF CORPORATIONS

An important advantage of the corporate structure is its continuity of operation that does not have to be affected by the death or retirement of individual shareholders. Even a sole-shareholder corporation can be sold in such a manner as to continue operations under the same name without interruption during the transition. Corporate stock that represents ownership rights is transferable to other persons or can be sold to another shareholder or newcomer to the business as a means of raising additional working capital. Two other advantages to the corporation's shareholders are centralized management and limited liability for corporate debt.

Some new business owners never pursue incorporation because they are discouraged by the complex paperwork necessary to begin operations and by the additional reporting requirements that occur regularly, such as corporate minutes, income tax filing, and other reports required by each state. Also, expenses for legal advice about the operation of the corporation do not end after the initial documents are completed; the need for up-to-date legal advice is ongoing. Another disadvantage of the corporate structure is that bringing in more shareholders may raise capital but dilute control of the founding shareholder(s).

A final disadvantage is that the shareholder's liability may not be limited to his or her investment in the corporation. A corporation may be recognized as an artificial person, but it takes the signature of a real person to handle its financial transactions. Thus, lease contracts and business loans made to a corporation usually require a personal guarantee by the majority shareholder.

TRANSFERRING CORPORATE STOCK AT RETIREMENT OR DEATH

From a legal perspective, a corporation's existence is limitless; you will see that existence referred to in documents as *in perpetuity*. However, few corporations have such a long life. In a small corporation, the retirement or death of the sole shareholder or majority shareholder spells the end of that business unless a buyer for the stock is ready and willing to purchase the corporation. Perhaps a minority shareholder or an associate counselor expresses an interest in continuing the practice. Such a situation is easy to handle if a buy-sell agreement is in force. This agreement provides for a stock purchase with or without a life insurance payout in a manner that is similar to that of the partnership buy-sell agreement already discussed. It allows the majority shareholder or surviving family member to liquidate corporate stock for cash (from insurance proceeds). This person gets the benefit of stepping into an ongoing business with less cash out of pocket (insurance premiums) than would otherwise be needed to purchase the stock. All parties benefit and the business continues to operate.

A well-drafted buy-sell agreement also establishes a method for valuation of the stock, easing what could otherwise become a major hurdle. Don't be surprised if you never totally understand the complex matters of stock rights, ownership, and valuation for small corporations as there is no simple way to explain these issues that are mired in tax code rules and legal verbiage; but do be sure that your accountant and attorney understand them. This is the stuff that fills volumes of tax law texts. The most important point for you to remember is that if your corporation fails to set a method for determining stock value, the IRS will do it for you. And it does not take an MBA to figure out who will be the big winner in that situation (answer: the IRS).

INFORMAL STRUCTURE: SOLE PROPRIETORSHIP

After making the break from full-time employment, most counselors begin their own business as self-employed sole proprietors. The sole proprietorship is the simplest form of business organization that has no existence apart from you, the owner.[3] So close is the tie that links you to your business that your personal assets are fully at risk for any business liabilities. From a financial and legal perspective, you and your business are inseparable. Starting a sole proprietorship is relatively simple and much less expensive than establishing a partnership or corporation.

ADVANTAGES AND DISADVANTAGES

The primary advantage of doing business as a sole proprietor is the ease with which you can begin, change, or cease operations without costs for filing fees (as with a corporation) or legal expenses to draft working agreements (as with a partnership). Decisions related to the business can be made simply, without consulting a board of directors or other partners. Reporting requirements are minimal; basically you need to file Schedule C for income taxes and pay the appropriate self-employment taxes. You don't even have to file a separate tax return. Just attach a Schedule C (*Profit and Loss from Business*) and Schedule SE (*Self-Employment Tax*) to your personal tax return. With less time spent doing the reporting and other business paperwork that is required in formal structures, you can devote more attention to counseling and to the management of your sole proprietorship.

However, there are some disadvantages to operating as a sole proprietorship, such as the unlimited liability for business problems that can threaten your personal financial security if your personal assets are attached by creditors to cover business debts. Another disadvantage is that you have no stock or ownership interests to sell so you must raise business start-up capital from your own assets or personally pledge for a loan to fund the business. In a sole proprietorship, since you bear the full burden of management and marketing decisions, ineffective service to clients or the ultimate failure of the business will be closely identified with you as an individual.

AN OPERATING PLAN FOR YOUR SOLE PROPRIETORSHIP

Astute sole proprietors go one step further than is required by law—they make an operating plan that is similar to a partnership agreement but designed for the sole proprietor. Now before you dismiss this as a trivial task, consider the benefits. The sole proprietor is both boss and employee, a dual and occasionally conflicting role. You can make that role more manageable by setting up some operational guidelines as to how you will fill your employee role and how you will carry out your administrative role. Isolate those tasks that are essential (such as bookkeeping and typing reports) but that can be delegated to a part-time or temporary employee. The operating plan can specify which tasks you will perform and which will be done by others.

By its very nature, counseling is a time-intensive business. So accept the fact that as your practice grows the time you once had available for administrative, secretarial, and custodial duties will diminish. An operating plan can help you determine alternatives for handling the administrative demands of running a sole proprietorship. At some point you may decide to hire counselor-employees or support staff while still remaining a sole proprietor. You may also review your practice for a possible change in structure to a corporation or partnership. Before you rush to make such a major change, however, remember the old saying, "If it ain't broke, don't fix it." You may not necessarily improve your practice by changing its business structure. Instead, consider ways to revise your operating plan for more efficient use of your time, employee time, and other resources. Fine tuning is much easier and less expensive than a total overhaul.

Associate with Other Professionals

Even bare-bones start-up expenses exceed the budget of some counselors who desire to have their own practices. A popular way to open a personal practice with reduced financial risk is to work as an associate in the office of another professional. This can be a mutually beneficial situation if the working relationship is well planned in advance. For example, a Christian psychiatrist or psychologist may agree to rent office space to a Christian mental health counselor. The counselor may work only on referrals or on a combination of referrals and personal contacts. In another scenario, a counselor may lease more office space than is necessary and may feel financial pressure to cover the monthly rent by subleasing offices to other self-employed counselors. By working under these circumstances the self-employed counselor can avoid major office overhead expenses. In fact, having a counselor available to help patients cope with the emotional issues related to medical treatment is a growing trend among physicians, medical clinics, chiropractors, and physical therapists. Such an arrangement gives another dimension of service to the existing practice and encourages patient loyalty.

An Operating Agreement for an Association with Another Professional

There is more to making this association work than moving in your books and occupying an office. You need an operating agreement to spell out the duties and responsibilities of this business relationship. You will need to determine whether your relationship will resemble that of landlord-tenant or that of supervisor-associate. Will you be allowed to function as a true independent contractor (see chapter 9), or will you be treated as an unofficial employee? In your eagerness to get inexpensive office space and potential referrals, don't trip on any of the strings attached.

These important questions need to be resolved in the operating agreement between you and the professional whose office you propose to share:

1. What days or hours can the office space be used?

2. Is the use of common areas such as the reception room, kitchen, group room, or testing room included?

3. Is the office you are assigned already furnished, or can you decorate and bring furniture of your choice?

4. Can your business cards, brochures, and other marketing information be placed in common areas?

5. Will your name appear on the door or on the exterior business sign?

6. Can you use the office for seminars or groups during evening hours or weekends?

7. Will the receptionist answer your calls and schedule appointments, or are you responsible for these duties?

8. Is insurance billing provided or available for a fee?

9. What are the office rules of conduct? (i.e., no smoking, no unsupervised children in the waiting room, no coffee or colas in carpeted rooms)?

10. Can you obtain supervision or consultation from other professionals in the office?

11. What control, if any, is exercised by the professional over the work of the associates?

12. What are the causes and the period of notice required to terminate the association?

Any additional questions that you have about how to conduct your practice within the office of another professional need to be included in the operating agreement. Establish the terms of your relationship in writing and you will reduce the potential for misunderstanding in the future.

Sublease Agreement

If the business relationship is between you and the professional who holds the master lease for the office, then the connection is merely as a landlord-tenant governed by a sublease agreement. Bear in mind that an office sublease involves a contract obligating you to fulfill mutually acceptable terms or face monetary penalties. With that in mind, don't glance at it casually and sign quickly. Have your attorney review the sublease and a copy of the master lease to be certain that your interests are protected. Generally, a building owner reserves the right to give permission for any tenants to sublease to others. Just in case the current office occupant has failed to communicate with the building owner, a request from your attorney to see the master lease will settle the matter.

Some of the questions noted in the previous section on operating agreements may become part of your sublease agreement. If the sublease you are offered is too generic, your attorney can prepare changes that will tailor the agreement to fit your proposed use.

Whether you pay a monthly rent for regular use of an office or a weekly or daily rate for part-time use, be sure the sublease agreement clearly specifies the days or hours that you may occupy the office or any common areas. It is not unusual for a spare office to be leased to two or three different counselors. The office you lease during the day on Monday and Wednesday, may be leased to a second counselor for day hours on Tuesday and Thursday, and to a third counselor for evening hours on Monday, Tuesday, and Thursday. To prevent schedule conflicts and disagreements, know exactly when you have exclusive rights to occupy the office.

Another factor to consider in such a situation is that subleasing an office involves more than sharing space; it involves sharing a reputation. Even if your counseling practice operates independently of the professional from whom you sublet, your clients will perceive your presence there as a sanction of all the practitioners in the office. Remember this wise biblical advice. "Do not be yoked together with unbelievers. For what do righteousness and wickedness have in common? Or what fellowship can light have with darkness?" (2 Cor. 6:14). Christian counselors must take care that their witness is not tarnished by the behaviors or therapeutic styles of ungodly office mates.

FEE SHARING AND REFERRAL FEES

You might be offered an office-sharing arrangement with reduced rent in return for a pledge of fee sharing or referral fees. Under some state laws and professional codes this is the "free lunch" that you pay for with your license to practice. Never assume that the person whose office you propose to share is current on the regulations that govern your license status, even if that person is licensed under the same statute you are. Ask for written substantiation (copy of the statute or code of ethics) that affirms these fees as acceptable.

Fee sharing is actually a percentage split of the gross fee. Instead of a flat-rate rental, a counselor might pay a percentage of the total fees collected as rent. In a full-service office this fee will include secretarial services, billing, and clinical supervision. The split can range from seventy-thirty to fifty-fifty with the larger amount payable as rent. An office with fewer services or a counselor with a steady flow of clients may negotiate payments down to 40 percent. During the early days of building a practice, fee sharing allows the counselor to pay for space as used. Later, however, as the practice grows, a high fee split favors the landlord. If your appointment schedule is full and your collection rate is consistently high, paying more than 40 percent for office rent plus other operating expenses such as marketing and billing is an unacceptable rate.

Referral fees or any attempt to disguise them raises ethical questions. In Florida, as in some other states, the issue is settled by law, which forbids "paying or receiving a kickback, rebate, bonus or other remuneration for receiving a patient or client or referring a patient or client to another provider of mental healthcare services or goods; or entering into a reciprocal referral agreement."[4] The penalty for violating this rule in Florida is both a reprimand and a monetary fine. Check your state statutes or code of ethics for any rules regarding referral fees. Then give yourself a personal ethics check based on these two criteria: (1) referrals need to be made on the basis of your best professional judgment that the client is beyond your ability to provide service and will benefit from the referral; (2) financial gain is not an appropriate criterion for referral decisions. Scripture reminds us to be "not greedy for money, but eager to serve" (1 Pet. 5:2). So, as a closing admonition, remember that with the flaws inherent in our humanity, referral fees can easily obscure professional judgment.

NOTES

1. *Tax Guide for Small Business,* Internal Revenue Service Publication 334, revised November 1992, 115
2. Ibid., 17
3. Ibid., 4
4. Florida Statutes Chapter 21CC-5.001 (j) Discipline Guidelines, revised June 1992.

Chapter Four

The Church-Linked Counseling Practice

For God's gifts and his call are irrevocable.

Romans 11:29

SETTING UP A NONPROFIT CORPORATION UNDER IRS 501(c)(3)

SOME HARD-WORKING ENTREPRENEURS will tell you that they are running a nonprofit business, but not by choice! Actually a true nonprofit corporation is not one that fails to make money, nor is it always small and struggling. There are many examples of national and local nonprofit organizations and ministries that are as successful in fund-raising, money management, and delivery of services as any for-profit corporation. Essentially a nonprofit corporation does not pursue money (profit) as a major goal or have the need to keep shareholders satisfied with fat dividend checks as regular corporations do.

Twenty-three types of organizations can apply for exemption from federal income tax under Section 501(c) of the Internal Revenue Code. The complete list with appropriate code references is printed in IRS Publication 557, *Tax Exempt Status for Your Organization.* Your church-linked counseling ministry is likely to qualify under section 501(c)(3), which applies to

"religious, educational, charitable, scientific, literary organizations." A counseling ministry that serves as a department of
the church may not have separate incorporation or tax status.
In this arrangement, the church and its deacon board deal with
the organizational matters as part of the church governance.
Other church-linked counseling ministries operate as a separate business structure. The incorporation and tax exemption
procedures that follow in this chapter are directed at these
types of counseling services.

Articles of Incorporation

The formative stages for nonprofit corporations are similar
to those of regular corporations. The first step is to draft the
articles of incorporation, including the organization's name,
location, name of the registered agent, and the statement that
the corporation is established "in perpetuity." If you plan to
seek IRS 501(c)(3) approval as a tax-exempt organization, the
articles must include several statements that are specific to
nonprofits. The following information provides only a brief
overview of the required statements. We advise that you consult with your attorney for the final drafting language.

The articles must include a statement that the organization's
purpose is "exclusively for charitable, religious, educational,
and scientific purposes, including the making of distributions
to organizations that qualify as exempt organizations under
section 501(c)(3) of the Internal Revenue Code or corresponding section of any future federal tax code."[1]

Another article is required to stipulate that "no part of net
earnings shall inure to the benefit of, or be distributed to its
members, trustees, officers or other private persons, except that
the corporation shall be authorized and empowered to pay reasonable compensation for services rendered."[2] This article goes
on to forbid engaging in propaganda efforts in order to influence legislation or to participate in political campaigns.
Otherwise the corporation may carry on any activities and accept contributions as long as these pursuits are in compliance
with the federal tax code.

A provision for dissolving the nonprofit corporation must
be detailed within the articles of incorporation. This is to prevent

a tax-exempt organization from raising funds and then dissolving the corporation so that the directors or trustees can "take the money and run." The assets and funds raised by a tax-exempt organization are "permanently dedicated to an exempt purpose."[3] When a tax-exempt organization is dissolved, the remaining funds and assets must be "distributed for one or more exempt purposes within the meaning of section 501(c)(3) or be distributed by a Court of Competent Jurisdiction."[4] The court is intended to be within the same county as the headquarters of the defunct organization in order to allow the funds to remain in the same community and to be used for comparable charitable purposes. An alternative is to distribute the assets to the federal, state, or local government for use in a public program.

Nonprofit corporations do not have capital stock; hence, there are no shareholders. Instead, the corporation is governed by directors or trustees who have a fiduciary or pastoral interest in the management and continuation of the organization. Directors are granted limited liability under the articles, however, they may still be liable for negligence or fraud related to the performance of their duties to the corporation.

The second step is to file the articles of incorporation with the state in which the corporation's principal office is located. A filing fee is charged for this service. For a small additional fee, you may order a certified copy of the articles, which is useful in financial transactions and in legal matters. If you have not called the state division of corporations to request a name search prior to filing the articles, it is advisable not to print stationery until you are certain that the corporation name you have chosen is available. If the name you have chosen includes part of the name of your church or other ministry, your attorney will need to contact the other organization and obtain written approval to use its name. Be careful not to imply by clever acronyms or twist of words an affiliation with another ministry where such an affiliation does not formally exist.

BYLAWS

The bylaws of a nonprofit corporation define how the organization will operate from an administrative perspective. In essence, the bylaws contain both the brakes and the accelerator to keep your organization on course: safeguards to prevent gridlock by the board of directors and provisions to facilitate changes that are in accord with the organization's mission statement. The bylaws need to be written with enough detail to serve as the active governing document for the organization.

The bylaws include a specific description of how the organization plans to fulfill its mission statement. For example, if your nonprofit counseling center operates for charitable purposes, you will need to stipulate exactly what services will be rendered. To avoid being too restrictive, you might indicate that the purposes of the corporation include but are not limited to those services you describe. Ask your attorney to review this section carefully to be certain that you have not inadvertently exceeded the bounds of what the IRS determines is a charitable purpose. A nonprofit organization engaging in activities that create "unrelated business income" not only brings tax problems to an otherwise tax-exempt organization, but demonstrates a movement that is operating outside the bounds of charitable intent. (For more information on unrelated business income see chapter 9.)

Does your nonprofit organization grant membership to persons outside of the board of directors? If so, the criteria for membership must be clearly stated in the bylaws. This includes information on who may qualify for membership, how members are selected, the length of membership, and the rights and privileges of membership.

The job descriptions for the board of directors or trustees who form the governing body of the nonprofit corporation are to be included in the bylaws. The minimum number of directors or trustees in active service at any given time must comply with rules set by the state in which your organization is incorporated. In addition, the bylaws must define how directors are selected, the length of their terms, any type of compensation or expenses to be paid to them, the procedure to fill a vacancy due to resignation or death, and the procedure for removing a director prior to the completion of his or her term. But be cautious when you are determining the amounts and types of compensation or expenses in your bylaws; be certain that directors' compensation or expense reimbursement is not in conflict with your state laws for nonprofit corporations. Remember, you will have to disclose this information to the IRS in applying for tax-exempt status.

To minimize the impact of the adjustment period as new members come onto the board, some organizations stagger terms so that only one-third of the membership changes at each election. With this system, the remaining members are familiar with the organization's business and can mentor new members in their involvement.

Job descriptions for corporate officers also need to be written in the bylaws. If your organization has a president, vice-president, secretary, and treasurer, the duties and powers granted to each position must be clearly defined. Additional information is required to explain how officers are elected, the length of their terms, and the procedures for replacing officers due to resignation or death and for removing an officer before his or her elected term ends.

As with any corporation, nonprofits must stipulate in their bylaws the minimum number of required meetings to be held during the year and the provisions for special meetings. The complexities of voting, proxies, quorums, establishing committees, amending the bylaws, and other procedural issues also need to be clarified. Here's where assistance from an attorney who is familiar with nonprofit corporation governing procedures can help you avoid creating a disaster of too many or too few rules of order.

In our modern, litigation-prone environment, nonprofit organizations need to offer some type of liability coverage for their boards of directors. In fact, some high-profile business and professional people have such high risks to deal with in their own businesses that they will not serve on a board unless liability coverage is provided by the organization. Discuss this coverage with your professional liability insurance carrier and with your local insurance agent. You can also get useful information by talking with the board chairpersons of established local colleges and charitable organizations about the coverage they provide for their board members. Unless your nonprofit organization provides board members with liability protection, you will have a difficult time getting distinguished community, civic, and church leaders to serve on your board of directors.

Gaining IRS Approval

With regard to gaining approval from the Internal Revenue Service, the most important thing to understand is that filing for nonprofit corporation status in your state does not automatically make your business tax-exempt from the IRS's viewpoint. Incorporation and tax exemption are separate processes. It is possible to operate as a nonprofit corporation within your state's laws and never qualify as a tax-exempt organization. Acceptance of a nonprofit corporation is granted by the state in which the articles of incorporation are filed. Approval of tax-exempt status is granted by the Internal Revenue Service and any applicable state taxing authority. These procedures are complementary but are not interchangeable. We stress this point because a great deal of confusion exists about the differences between nonprofit corporations and tax-exempt corporations.

To proceed with this filing, you need Form 1023, *Application for Recognition of Exemption Under Section 501(c)(3)* and Form 8718—*User Fee for Exempt Organization Determination Letter Request*. The application form is lengthy and demands detailed information about the organization's activities, sources of financial support, types of fund-raising, names of members of the governing body, and the extent of accountability or control exercised by any other organization (such as a sponsoring church). The following five required inclusions must be submitted with your application:[5]

1. Employer identification number.

2. Organizing documents, including a "conformed copy" of the articles of incorporation and bylaws.

3. A detailed description of the organization's purposes and activities as well as the "standards, criteria, and procedures for carrying out those purposes."

4. Complete financial statements for the current year (and three preceding years for existing organizations). New

organizations (less than one year in operation) must submit a budget for two accounting periods plus a list of current assets and liabilities. The source of funds must be indicated as public or private; this includes income from services, contributions, grants, or other clearly defined activities.

5. Fund-raising plans must be explained in "sufficient detail to show how your activities will be financed." You will also be asked whether fund-raising is handled by volunteers or by paid professional fund-raisers.

Item 2 refers to a conformed copy, which is a complete copy of the original document and any amendments. A corporate officer must sign to certify that the copy is an exact duplicate of the original. The certification statement must accompany a cover letter on your organization's letterhead or it may be typed on the last page of the copy. Here is an example: "This is a true and correct copy of the Articles of Incorporation of XYZ Corporation (name of your organization) that was filed with the state of (name) and registered on (date)." Or alter the wording to reflect the type of document: "This is a true and correct copy of the bylaws of XYZ Corporation (name of your organization) as adopted by the board of directors at the meeting on (date)." Your attorney will advise you if any special wording is necessary to validate the conformed copies.

Remember that all questions on the application must be answered in detail with no sweeping generalizations. It is not an essay test that can be inflated with meaningless words. However, if you have a valid answer that happens to need more space than the blank provided, you may continue the answer on an attached page by referencing the number of the question. To be certain the reader knows you have more to say, mark "see attachment" on the application. Every attached page must be 8 1/2 x 11 inches and must contain the organization's name, address, and employer identification number.

The other required form will indicate how much you have to pay as a *user fee* to the government for processing an exempt organization determination letter. Current fees range from $150 to $500. The lower fee applies to organizations with annual gross receipts below $10,000 in the last four tax years, or for a new organization that is not expected to exceed that amount in receipts for the first four operational years. Organizations with receipts or expectation of receipts in excess of $10,000 annually pay a $375 fee. Group exemption letters require a $500 fee. There is a space at the bottom of the form to attach your check or money order for the applicable fee. This completed form must be attached to the application.

After reviewing the application and supporting documents, the IRS sends a determination letter or makes a ruling to grant tax-exempt status. That status may be effective retroactive to the date the organization was formed or it may begin on a date stated in the letter or ruling. Failure to provide complete information or to qualify according to purpose and activities can result in an adverse determination or denial. However, you do have the right to appeal an adverse determination, which can occur for such a simple problem as failing to give a complete answer to a question. Such an error is easily corrected and you still have the ability to obtain tax-exempt status after making the necessary corrections. Before deciding to appeal on more difficult issues, however, consult both your accountant and an attorney with expertise in tax law.

After clearing the IRS hurdles to obtain tax-exempt status, you will need to apply for state income tax exemption and state sales tax exemption. Contact your state department of revenue for information on the forms and procedures necessary to obtain the applicable exemptions. To protect citizens from phony charitable solicitations, many state and local governments issue licenses or some form of registration for qualified charities. Ask your attorney to review and recommend implementation procedures for any and all registrations necessary to grant your tax-exempt organization full rights to raise funds and engage in all lawful activities.

The processes for achieving nonprofit incorporation status and tax-exemption are complex, and by no means is this book intended as a "starter kit" for do-it-yourselfers. Since the errors and omissions made by novices can cause long delays and sometimes result in denial, make certain you seek advice from an attorney with experience in representing nonprofit corporations.

In addition, talk with administrators and founding board members of other nonprofit organizations in your community to ask about their wisest decisions and their most frustrating problems in securing all the proper clearances to begin their organizations or ministries. One thing you are bound to hear is that the paperwork is awesome.

Defining the Church-Counseling Link

The call to counsel is a call to serve. Some ministers receive the call to counsel as part of their pastoral duties while other men and women are called to counsel as a profession, apart from an ordained ministry yet very much a ministry of service whether conducted inside or outside the church. It is another example of the wonderful diversity that exists in the body of Christ. "There are different kinds of gifts, but the same Spirit. There are different kinds of service, but the same Lord. There are different kinds of working, but the same God works all of them in all men" (1 Cor. 12:4–6). Let's look at three different models of counseling practice that exist in close relationship with a local church.

Model 1. Counseling as a Department in the Church

As the demand increases for more than occasional counseling, a church may respond to that need by creating a ministry within the ministry devoted exclusively to counseling. Larger churches often have a minister of counseling whose full-time job is to counsel or to serve as the counselor-administrator of other trained counselors or lay counselors who work with the congregation.

When it developes as a department of the local church, the counseling ministry forms a unique partnership with the church's other designated ministries. Since emotional problems never discriminate by age or life stage, the pastor in each department is often the first to counsel with a troubled individual or family. Then, when the complexities of the problem or the time it consumes begins to overwhelm the pastor, the individual or family is referred to the minister of counseling. In such a situation it is crucial to develop an understanding and to set some ground rules about when to refer. The senior pastor can lead by example in showing that a counseling ministry enhances, never diminishes, the pastoral role. Even subtle feelings of competition between the counselor and various pastors need to be recognized and dealt with honestly. In time, an effective counseling ministry proves to be a blessing to the staff and the church family.

A counseling department functioning within the local church simply assumes a place on the organizational chart of the existing operational structure. The minister of counseling may report directly to the senior pastor or to the pastoral administrator. Some departmental guidelines may be established for setting appointments, fees (if any), types of counseling offered, and supervision of cases. If the minister of counseling is not a licensed professional counselor, be certain that the services offered as a pastoral counselor do not cross state laws regulating the practice of marriage and family therapy or mental health counseling. As a means of accountability, the minister of counseling needs a group of licensed Christian counselors and psychologists who are willing to serve as advisers and accept referrals for evaluation. This consultation approach safeguards the interest of the client and can reduce the church's liability.

The church needs to establish a continuing-education budget so that the minister of counseling and lay counselors receive regular training. Call on Christian professional counselors from your congregation and the community to conduct monthly (or no less than quarterly) in-service training for the church counseling staff. In addition, the church can provide both education and a time of recommitment by sponsoring their counselors' attendance at high-quality Christian conferences such as those sponsored by the American Association of Christian Counselors (AACC) and the Christian Association for Psychological Studies (CAPS).

There are advantages to providing counseling as a department in the church; these include the fact that (1) no new corporation or business structure is required, (2) church facilities are available for use at no extra expense, and (3) church members have the convenience of a Christian counseling service at the church.

Some disadvantages of counseling as a department in the church include the problem that church offices are rarely soundproof, which may compromise confidentiality, and the possibility that the minister of counseling may have other pastoral duties that limit the available time and attention that individual can give to counseling clients.

Model 2. A Separate Counseling Ministry within a Shared Facility

A somewhat different approach is the church counseling center that remains on the church grounds and under the spiritual leadership of the church, yet, maintains separate operational control. This situation is similar to a bookstore or elementary school that is located on church property but functions as a separate yet connected ministry.

Such a counseling center brings a biblically based service to church members, but it can be much more. This is a unique opportunity for evangelism by demonstrating to the nonbelievers in the community that Christians are concerned for their emotional problems as well as for their spiritual needs. If your church wants to open the counseling center to the community, it would be helpful to consider choosing a different name from that of the church to give it an individual identity. You will attract more nonbelievers and persons from other churches by welcoming these clients into the counseling center whether or not they actively participate in any church.

Clients need to know that if they seek counseling at the church center they will not be proselytized or absorbed into the sponsoring church against their will. Many clients would avoid counseling if they felt such a commitment was involved; they simply are not ready for that step. Thus, a name that does not imply church affiliation is less threatening to these persons. Instead of "First Church of ABC Counseling Center" create a name that is appropriate to your mission statement such as "New Hope Counseling Center" or "Family Recovery Center."[6] Whether or not you choose to incorporate the center, call the state division of corporations and ask for a name search of existing nonprofit corporations. In brainstorming ideas for names, write down all possible suggestions and try these in different combinations. But be careful not to be too clever and avoid using a name (an Old Testament spelling for example) that would be difficult to remember or find in the phone directory.

If at all possible, select a location on the church property that has an outside entrance. Some clients are intimidated by having to walk through the sanctuary or pastoral offices. Also, since many counseling sessions take place in the evening, a separate entrance is more easily monitored for security. Place the center's name on the door or on a prominent sign at or near the door. If city sign ordinances permit, get a separate sign for the counseling center at the location most visible to traffic. If parking is limited, place signs reserving several nearby spaces for counseling center clients (including both handicapped and regular parking spaces).

To serve as director of the center, you will probably want a counselor-administrator: someone with both counselor training and people-management skills who can relate to clients, counseling staff, and the church administrator. Although the counseling center maintains its own director, support staff, and advisory board, the director may be given a department head position within the church staff. This is like the divisions of a commercial corporation in which a department is given substantial internal control yet remains accountable to the corporate headquarters.

Offering services to the public outside your congregation stretches the limits of pastoral connections, so you will need to check your state counseling laws carefully as they relate both to the types of services offered and to the requirements that are necessary to provide those services to the public. In numerous states, pastoral counseling conducted with congregation members has greater latitude than that involving nonmembers. Also, most state laws regulate the practice of mental health counseling and hold individual counselors to that standard regardless of the claim to be simply a pastoral counselor. However, it may be possible to expand your center's services in the community by having one or more licensed Christian counselors on staff. If your state law permits, a licensed counselor may be allowed to function as the clinical supervisor of the other nonlicensed or pastoral counselors.

The advantages of a separate counseling center within a shared facility include having an individual identity in the community but with the authority to establish internal staff controls that safeguard confidentiality. As part of a working relationship with the church, the counseling center saves rental expenses by using a wing or a building on the church property for office space and has availability of the church auditorium or conference rooms for group counseling and special programs. Money saved on rental and maintenance can be used to provide more counseling services. The separate counseling center builds its own reputation and outreach programs to serve both the congregation and the community (evangelism outreach).

While the advantages are appealing, this arrangement also has some disadvantages. So often the opening ceremony for a new church building is hardly over before every new space is filled and the pastor starts having nightmares of yet another building program. This can be a problem for the separate counseling center within the shared facility because its expansion space may be limited and it will have to compete with other departments for budget needs. As mentioned earlier, another problem is that church offices are rarely soundproof and the walls may not be suitable for reinforcing to ensure confidentiality. Another problem can occur when church programs and counseling group sessions occur simultaneously and the parking lot overflows. Also, if the counselor-administrator serves as the center's liaison with the church administration, he or she has to spend additional time away from counseling to interact with other pastors and the church board.

MODEL 3. COUNSELING IN A SEPARATE LOCATION, WITH SEPARATE CONTROL, IN A COVENANT RELATIONSHIP WITH THE SPONSORING CHURCH

This model serves as an expansion plan for centers that have outgrown operations in a shared facility. Sometimes this type of counseling ministry begins as God's call to an individual, then gains the attention and sponsorship of one or more local churches. In either case, this counseling center progresses through the same developmental stages as any new business.

As an autonomous ministry, the center is responsible for its own organization, administration, financing, and staff. Rather than being a department of the church, the counseling center affirms a covenantal relationship with the sponsoring church, denomination, or coalition of churches. The covenantal bond is secure yet flexible, like the new kind of relationship that emerges between parents and their adult children. A formal document detailing the nature of the covenant relationship needs to be drafted, signed, and regularly reviewed. The document must specify whether the sponsoring church's influence is spiritual, administrative, financial, or some combination of those. Having a strong church as a spiritual anchor is a great asset to a counseling center.

The governing processes of the center will be defined within its nonprofit corporation bylaws. A counselor-administrator directs the staff and works with the board of directors. By choosing board members with business, financial, management, and healthcare backgrounds the center gains added expertise that would otherwise be costly to hire. However, the assistance from board members must always be in addition to, and not a replacement for, a team of professional advisers (see chapter 5).

The independent counseling center also needs an advisory group of church members and other Christians in the community. These advisers serve as a focus group of eight to ten people that keeps the center aware of concerns of various ages and special interest groups within the church and the community (see chapter 6). One lay adviser represents each segment of the counseling clients such as singles, married couples, working women and men, or senior adults. If your clients are referred from several local churches, consider inviting some members of other churches to be part of your advisory group. Or have two advisory groups: one composed of members from your church and the other of members from other churches in the community.

In developing a business plan, the counseling center will define its primary and secondary target clients from within the community. Church referrals are not always enough to sustain the budget of an independent office. Furthermore, the counseling center can take advantage of its location to attract clients from nearby offices or neighborhoods. Find the most visible, attractive office location that you can comfortably afford. The ability to have an on-street sign or a bold sign on your building will help to draw clients. Do as much as the city ordinances or office complex rules permit to call attention to your center.

Obtaining tax-exempt status is important to your independent, nonprofit counseling center. The financial support given by the church may not increase as rapidly as your expenses. Other changes in the church's priorities can cause a reduction in the amount allocated for sponsorship. Your center needs a plan to supplement church support with at least one major annual fund-raising campaign.

In using this model, you are essentially an entrepreneur with all the startup and management demands of any new business. While the church link offers financial and prayer support, from a business and legal perspective your center is a stand-alone ministry. The possibilities that result from this awareness are both humbling and exciting.

The advantages of an independent counseling center in covenant with a sponsoring church include: (1) the opportunity to establish an individual identity in the community, (2) the authority to establish internal staff controls to protect client confidentiality, and (3) autonomy of operation. Furthermore, the independent center has the opportunity to attract qualified counselors and staff from other churches and denominations that share complementary biblical counseling approaches. An added advantage is that the tax-exempt status can be a significant help in soliciting private contributions and planning community-based fund-raisers to supplement or increase the operational budget.

However, as attractive as independence seems, there are disadvantages. Once the counseling center goes out on its own it is fully responsible for operational costs (with or without church support). An independent counseling center faces some of the same disadvantages as a private practice in that it is subject to financial pressures from the local economy, and it must build a faithful donor base or collect enough fees to remain in operation. If the center policies stray too far from the original covenant, the sponsoring church may withhold financial support. Other disadvantages include the fact that the center's director and some staff members will have to handle both counseling and administrative functions. In addition, once the center moves off church property, there are fewer opportunities for the counselors to have regular fellowship with pastors and church staff.

Independent Counselor in a Church-Linked Ministry

There is yet another way to link the church and counseling in a less formal arrangement than that of the three counseling models. An alternative is for the church to contract with a licensed professional counselor for part-time services offered at the church. This is a highly cost-efficient option for a smaller church that cannot afford either the salary of another minister or the facilities and staff to run a counseling center. It is an equally attractive option for medium to large churches that desire to have both Christian professional counseling and pastoral counseling available to members.

This is a relatively simple option to implement. Once an agreement is signed, the church merely sets up a quiet, comfortable, and private room for counseling. The mental health professional is responsible for his or her own liability coverage, insurance billing, collections, appointment schedules, and management of counseling cases. In other words, the church provides office space and referrals; the counselor does the rest.

Operating Agreement or Employment Agreement with a Church

The relationship between a church and an independent counselor works best when an agreement is made that defines how this alliance will operate for mutual benefit. If the counselor has substantial control over the days, times, fees, and methods of his or her work, he or she may qualify as an independent contractor. Carefully review all twenty factors that pertain to this determination, as presented in chapter 9. However, even if the counselor's agreement with the church is fairly open-ended, the "continuing nature of the relationship" (factor 6) threatens the independent contractor status. Have your attorney and accountant review this problem carefully as it pertains both to contract terms and IRS matters.

An employment agreement is more appropriate for a continuing relationship in which the church exercises control (factors 1, 3, 10, 11) and retains the right to dismiss the counselor (factor 19). Request that your attorney draft a combination operating agreement and employment agreement. In so doing, the church covers all necessary employment criteria and adds guidelines under which the counselor is allowed to use church property and accept church referrals. By mutual consent, the terms of employment for a counselor who spends one, two, or three days per week at a church can be different than that of full-time church employees.

As for payment, discuss with your attorney and accountant which of the commonly used methods of payment are acceptable: 1. Paying the counselor a daily rate for a certain number of hours, or 2. Allowing the counselor to keep all or part of the fees collected. The amount of additional bookkeeping time required varies according to the payment plan selected. However, payment based on fees generated by counseling is essentially self-supporting and not another drain on the church budget. If earned fees are the counselor's payment for services, the church may also pay a small monthly fee (equal to two to four counseling hours) to compensate the counselor for time spent working with no-pay referrals, assisting a pastor with crisis stabilization for a depressed or distraught church member, and consultations with the pastoral staff.

RATIO OF MINISTRY CLIENTS AND PRIVATE CLIENTS

An important issue to clarify in any working agreement with a contracted professional counselor is the degree of exclusivity of service that is expected by the church. Is the counselor only allowed to schedule appointments for church members while working on a given day at the church? Or can the counselor bring in private clients who are not members or referrals from the host church? If the counselor can schedule private clients, is there a percentage of time that the church wants reserved for its referrals? Almost any formula for scheduling is possible; however, the more church control that is added, the more a counselor's status as an employee is confirmed.

Settling contract and work status issues are always necessary before any work begins. Yet there is a sensitivity issue that must be addressed up front to establish positive rapport. The counselor and pastor (or pastoral staff) have to spend time thoroughly discussing how each of them views this new working relationship to avoid any future misunderstandings. The counselor must be careful not to overstep the authority of the pastor, and the pastor, likewise, must respect the counselor's professional competence. Both need to work at all costs to avoid any confusion over roles or responsibilities in this relationship through open, honest discussions. As a counselor, you know the danger of unspoken assumptions. To keep this pastor-counselor alliance, both of you must prayerfully seek God's blessing on this new phase of ministry and mutually pledge to continue the working relationship as it was formed—in a spirit of cooperation.

NOTES

1. *Tax-Exempt Status for Your Organization,* Internal Revenue Service Publication 557, revised January 1992, 13.
2. Ibid.
3. Ibid.
4. Ibid.
5. Ibid., 2
6. Names noted are fictitious and not representative of any known counseling center.

Chapter 5

The People Behind
Your Business

Plans fail for lack of counsel, but with many advisors they succeed.
Proverbs 15:22

LIKE COUNSELING CLIENTS, A COUNSELING business responds to the effects of external and internal changes. Externally, the practice is prey to competition, recession, adverse publicity, or even blocked entry to the parking lot due to road repairs. Internally, concerns include finding and retaining staff, handling collections, and sustaining quality controls. To meet predictable and unpredictable business problems, the counselor-administrator needs a team of advisers and associates to deal with the development, maintenance, and staffing of the counseling center.

DEVELOPING YOUR PRACTICE

The basic advisory team to bring your counseling center from planning into reality consists of an attorney, an accountant, a financial planner and an insurance agent. In selecting professionals to fill these roles, consider their expertise plus experience in working with small businesses or nonprofit organizations similar in size to your practice. You will gain double blessings from an adviser with academic and actual exposure to your management challenges. For ways to verify advisers' credentials, see Table 5.1

ATTORNEY

The business aspects of a counseling practice are subject to a host of legal parameters. If you fail to recognize the barriers or ignore the traps, you may find yourself stuck like a lab rat in a maze. Before any legal problems occur find a competent attorney. Too many new business owners dabble in do-it-yourself legal advice—a mistake that usually results in far greater costs to correct problems than would have been spent by working with an attorney to set up the practice properly in the beginning.

Look upon your attorney as your ally; bring him or her on your team early in the business-planning process. For many smaller counseling practices, a skilled general-practice attorney with community business and estate-planning experience is a good choice. Church-linked counseling centers operating as nonprofit corporations need an attorney who is knowledgeable in business, local laws, and tax law pertaining to 501(c)(3) organizations. A larger group counseling practice or one that plans to operate multiple counseling centers is better served by an experienced corporate attorney accustomed to dealing with more complex business structures.

Whether to retain an attorney with a major law firm or work with one or more individual practitioners is a difficult decision. A multi-discipline law firm offers specialists in business, taxes, estate planning, copyrights, worker's compensation, zoning, real estate, and litigation. This one-stop-shopping opportunity saves time and enhances coordination between your general business attorney and any of the firm's specialists who are needed for a particular problem. However, such convenience comes at a price that is not affordable for all circumstances. Major law firms frequently command higher fees and may require a retainer to be paid annually or quarterly. From your perspective as the client, the more favorable arrangement is with a retainer that serves as an advance payment for legal fees. Having a law firm on retainer to your counseling center gives you priority access as an existing client.

Another alternative for legal services is to work with a smaller legal group or sole practitioner. If that is your choice, seek a competent generalist who comes highly recommended by other business clients. This attorney will take the lead in providing you with basic legal and organizational advice. If specialists are needed, you will want your attorney to refer to and work with those specialists. Instead of one-stop-shopping, supplementary legal services may be purchased a la carte—an approach that can be less expensive and seldom requires on-going retainer fees. You also have the advantage of building a close working relationship with an attorney who is, like you, a small business manager.

Before making a final decision on which attorney or law firm to use, arrange a personal meeting with the top two or three candidates, because the level of rapport and trust between you and your attorney needs to be an important factor in the decision. Ask specific questions about the attorney's prior experience in representing professional or pastoral counselors. What does the attorney know about your state statutes regulating counselors or the statutory definition of "privileged communication"? Does this attorney feel capable of advising you about how to proceed if you or your clients' records are subpoenaed? Is the attorney willing to take time (not on your bill) to become familiar with the statutes governing your practice? If the attorney regularly works with healthcare or personal-service providers, he or she can translate that experience to comparable needs of a counseling practice.

Church-linked counseling centers may have at least one attorney in the congregation who is willing to provide legal advice without charge or at a reduced cost. Although the price is tempting, apply the same criteria just discussed when you make the final decion. The volunteer attorney may turn out to be a distinguished maritime or immigration specialist who is far removed from small business issues. How often do you expect errant ships or illegal aliens to pose threats to your counseling center? This volunteer professional might better serve as a board member who coordinates legal services rather than as the primary provider of business legal advice. Let him or her take the lead in finding and negotiating with a law firm or attorney who is better suited to working with business development. If an attorney within your congregation does have both the appropriate experience and the willingness to serve, say yes without delay!

ACCOUNTANT

If the conspicuous absence of math courses is what made liberal arts or seminary appealing to you, you can be sure you will be out of your range in business accounting. After all, accounting is a very detailed, mathematical method of maintaining accountability or demonstrating the true profit or loss position of your business with numbers. Scripture continually reminds us that we are accountable to God for our actions, and as a counselor-administrator, you are also accountable to yourself, to your associates, and possibly to a board of directors for the use of financial and time assets in your counseling practice. No wonder you need an accountant to select and implement a business records and payments system that will be functional, manageable, and capable of growing to meet future needs.

The level of expertise available for accounting tasks varies. The basic functions of posting, payments, and check reconciliation can be done by a bookkeeper. These tasks are often performed by the secretary or owner in a new or small business. However, you may prefer an external bookkeeping service, which often is available for a reasonable fee. In my area, several enterprising self-employed bookkeepers work by the delivery or drop-in methods. Either you deliver your books to the bookkeeper's home or office or the bookkeeper drops in to your office on a prearranged weekly or monthly schedule to do the work. You may be pleasantly surprised to find some very talented, corporate-trained bookkeepers who are choosing to work part-time while concentrating on other roles as a full-time parent or retiree. Look for notices of bookkeeping services in your community newspaper, church bulletin boards, or through senior adult service centers. And remember to ask other counselors or owners of personal-service businesses for their referrals to high-quality, efficient, and moderately priced bookkeeping services.

Yet, while keeping the basic bookkeeping up-to-date may get the bills paid and the checking account reconciled, it is far short of the complete financial analysis you need to develop and maintain a counseling practice. Your advisory team needs an accountant with analytical training and practical business experience. More than a "number cruncher," a skilled accountant saves you money by designing a manageable accounting system, identifying errors in financial statements or projections, monitoring collections, and maintaining compliance with local, state, and federal taxes. However, for more sophisticated analyses, audits, tax complications, or financing proposals for lenders, your business needs a certified public accountant (CPA). The CPA is a college graduate who has passed a rigorous qualifying exam covering all areas of professional accounting. From that point, some CPAs further specialize in working with certain types of businesses. On a hierarchy of service fees, you can expect CPA fees to be higher than those of accountants. So you will want to decide whether to choose a CPA or an accountant based on the size, scope, and financial complexity of your counseling practice.

In the search for a qualified accountant, like that for your attorney, take into consideration your personal preference for working with a large accounting firm or an independent accountant. The major firm, especially a big-name company, offers a wealth of in-house expertise on cost accounting, business development, tax planning, employee benefits, audits, and charitable organizations.

As much as the major firm has to offer, these may be more services and at a higher fee than your business requires. The smaller firm or self-employed accountant may have all the expertise your fledgling practice needs and at more affordable fees.

Whether you choose an accountant or a CPA from a small or large firm, these are important items to consider in choosing your accounting adviser:

- Training, experience, and credentials appropriate to the task
- Good recommendations from at least three successful local businesses

- His or her willingness to participate in the development of your business plan
- Experience in accounting systems for counselors or healthcare providers
- A cooperative attitude about working with other advisory team members
- Patience to teach you the essentials of your accounting system, including how to read and constructively use data from financial statements and reports

A church-linked counseling center will add to this list the preference for accounting experience with charitable organizations.

Financial Planner

Your personal and business finances are separate but equally important. As you carefully consider the risks and rewards of starting a counseling practice (see chapter 1), you will realize how delicate this financial balance becomes in a new business. This is an area where the expertise of a financial planner is invaluable to show you how to keep a balance between the dual nature of your financial life (business and personal).

Ideally, the financial planner is the first adviser you consult before making the decision whether to enter private or group practice or to launch a church-linked counseling center. A planner looks objectively at the assets, debts, income, investments, and projections for future needs to determine if your family or church can begin such a new venture responsibly.

There is a hierarchy of expertise in financial planning similar to that in accounting. Since "financial planner" is not a protected title, it is used (and misused) by stockbrokers, tax preparers, insurance salesmen, telephone solicitors, and others of dubious training. So you are on your own when you try to determine whether a financial planner is actually a "financial seller" looking for a kinder and gentler title. You may receive a "free" financial plan that is about as personal as a pair of one-size fits all socks. Or you may get pressure to spend your money (on recommended investments) disguised as planning. The test of a real financial planner is his or her demonstrated capability to review, comprehend, restructure, and show ways to improve your financial situation before anything gets bought or sold. Whether the planner gets paid by commissions only or by commissions plus fees, the intangible factors are ethics and experience. Always ask for a résumé listing both educational credentials and occupational experience. Then ask for references from two clients. These are likely to be satisfied clients, but the financial seller with no real planning experience would shy away from letting you talk to any former clients.

In contrast, the Certified Financial Planner and the Chartered Financial Consultant (ChFC)[1] set the standard of excellence by education, examination, ethics, and experience. Like the CPA, the CFP and ChFC titles are earned and sustained by annual continuing education. Trained in planning, insurance, investments, taxes, retirement plans, employee benefits, and estate planning, these specialists are qualified to offer a total-spectrum review to analyze and balance personal and business finances. Under strict codes of ethics, professional planners must give each client a comprehensive disclosure. This disclosure reveals educational background, experience, any conflicts of interest, methods and sources of compensation, and philosophy of personal financial planning. Compensation or payment for financial planning is rendered by one of three methods:

- Fee paid for planning services: hourly or base fee plus hourly charge for additional work.

- Commissions for investments with no additional charge for planning.

- Fee plus commissions: standard fees (hourly or per plan) charged separately (may or may not include commissions for investments or insurance products).

When working with an ethical professional, you can expect to receive answers to your questions about costs and level of services before the planning relationship begins. That disclosure, along with any recommendations of financial advisers given to you by friends or associates, is a solid basis on which to choose a financial planner for your advisory team.

Insurance Agent

Liability is an increasingly troublesome fact of life in personal service businesses like counseling. The extent of your exposure to claims goes beyond malpractice. In fact, you are probably at a greater risk of losing your business in a lawsuit initiated by a client who slips and falls in the reception room than by one who is unhappy with your counseling approach. Unfortunately, this is just one of the normal risks of opening your door to serve the public. Even churches are no longer immune. In some situations, a church-linked counseling center faces a higher risk of a lawsuit than a private practice because of the presumed "deep pockets," the expectation of claiming assets from the sponsoring church. If you want to practice counseling wisely, you cannot afford to ignore the potential financial risks of doing business. Thus you must either accept the risks (self-insure and pay losses out of pocket) or transfer the risks by initiating a risk-management program.

A qualified, state-licensed insurance agent knows how to look for potential risks and estimate the severity of losses. He or she then proposes coverage to offset losses and identifies ways to reduce your risks. Risk involves more than fire, theft, or injury. Losses that affect your business also result from your disability, hospitalization, or death. The former is covered by property and casualty insurance and the latter by life and health insurance. Some agents specialize in one of these areas, while others represent multi-line companies covering personal and business risks. You may choose to work with two agent specialists or with one multi-line agent.

If your agent is an employee or representative of only one company, you will be given one coverage package. The only way to compare costs is to get bids for similar coverage from other companies. Some agents work independently and are licensed with several companies. The independent agent can present high-, middle-, and low-cost options for comparable coverage.

Local agents are rarely able to offer affordable options for the malpractice (also known as errors and omissions) coverage that is necessary for counselors. Your best buy for this coverage comes through professional counselor organizations, pastoral groups, or denomination-sponsored insurance programs.

Insurance agents are licensed and regulated by state laws. Those laws also protect the consumer by requiring agents to give certain disclosures about the products and companies they represent. An elite group of agents have earned the designation CLU (Chartered Life Underwriter) or ChFC (Chartered Financial Consultant). These nationally recognized titles are earned by study at the American College in Bryn Mawr, Pennsylvania, and maintained through continuing education monitored by the American Society of CLU and ChFC. A CLU or ChFC is particularly well qualified to help you design, implement, and monitor a risk-management program.

Unless your agent offers advanced risk-management planning at a fee, the agent is compensated by commissions. These commissions are based on a percentage of the premium paid. It is similar to purchasing an airline ticket directly from the airline versus through a travel agent. You pay the same price for the ticket. However, by working with the travel agent you get the benefit of planning expertise and personal service. That's the way insurance works. You pay the same premium based on the coverage whether you pay the company directly or thorough an agent. The agent is compensated by the company to work for you. The most successful agents focus on client service and know that the commissions will follow. To find a qualified, client-oriented agent, ask other small-business owners or counselors to recommend agents who have provided them with conscientious service and affordable coverage.

SPECIAL BUSINESS ASSISTANCE

Just as Scripture admonishes us to "teach what is in accord with sound doctrine" (Titus 2:1), so the Service Corps of Retired Executives (SCORE) teaches sound business doctrine and success principles to aspiring entrepreneurs. These retired executives are matched in a mentoring relationship with new business owners. SCORE seminars and consultations are free, yet the quality of assistance is priceless. This is just one of many special services sponsored by the Small Business Administration (SBA), a federal program developed in the 1950s to encourage the development of new businesses. You might also want to check with your chamber of commerce and local college or university for seminars and courses on marketing, business plans, accounting, personnel management, and other topics that would help you to more effectively develop and manage your counseling practice.

Development Team Transitions

The work of your development team does not end when you open the doors for business. Your attorney, accountant, financial planner, and insurance agent will continue to be involved, as needed, in future planning, growth, and periodic revaluation of the counseling center's progress. As you make changes or encounter potential risks, contact the appropriate advisers to evaluate the circumstances. Above all, don't try to do their jobs or second-guess their work if you aren't qualified. Let your advisers tend their areas of expertise, so you have more time and peace of mind to devote to counseling.

Table 5.1

How to Verify Professional Advisers' Credentials

Attorneys:
- American Bar Association, 750 N. Lake Shore Drive, Chicago, Illinois 60611. Telephone: 312-988-5000.
- Local or State Bar Associations: Check your local phone directory or call directory assistance in your state capital.
- Martindale-Hubbell Law Directory: Find this book in the reference section of your public library

Accountants:
- American Institute of Certified Public Accountants, 1211 Avenue of the Americas, New York, New York 10036. Telephone: 212-596-6200.
- National Society of Public Accountants, 1010 N. Fairfax Street, Alexandria, Virginia 22314. Telephone: 703-549-6400.

Financial Planners:
- International Board of Standards and Practices for Certified Financial Planners, 1660 Lincoln Street, #3050, Denver, Colorado 80264. Telephone: 303-830-7543.

Insurance Agents:
- State Insurance Commissioner: Call this office in your state capital to confirm an agent's license status.
- American Society of CLU and ChFC, 270 Bryn Mawr Avenue, Bryn Mawr, Pennsylvania 19010. Telephone: 215-526-2500.

Supervision/Consultation:
- State Department of Professional Regulation or Licensing Board for Professional Counselors: Consult your state capital.
- National Board of Certified Counselors (professional specialties), 3-D Terrace Way, Greensboro, North Carolina 27403. Telephone: 919-547-0607.

Marketing Consultants:
- Public Relations Society of America, 33 Irving Place, Third Floor, Fifteenth and Sixteenth Streets, New York, New York 10003. Telephone: 212-995-2230.

MAINTAINING YOUR PRACTICE

There is an old saying that the happiest day of a weekend sailor's life is the day he buys a boat—and the next happiest day is the day he sells the boat! What made the difference? Maintenance. The time and expenses of repairs and upkeep can take the wind out of the most devoted sailor. Your counseling practice also requires ongoing maintenance to function efficiently. But it doesn't have to be an overwhelming one-person chore. Support for this effort comes from your clinical supervisor, professional groups, billing service, and marketing consultant.

CLINICAL SUPERVISOR

Codes of ethical practice and many state laws require counselors to work under a licensed, experienced clinical supervisor. Licensed professional counselors have a responsibility to seek peer supervision or periodic review of their cases, and pastoral counselors are responsible to minister under the authority of their denomination or church governing board. Regardless of your status, operating as a "lone-ranger counselor" is dangerous and irresponsible. The counselor who seeks supervision acknowledges an obligation to be accountable and recognizes that "it is necessary to submit to the authorities, not only because of possible punishment but also because of conscience" (Rom. 13:5).

In a group practice or larger counseling center, the director or other appropriately qualified staff counselor may serve as clinical supervisor. A counselor working alone or within a church-linked ministry can contract with an experienced professional for supervision to serve as a supervisor. In fact, in some states an unlicensed counselor is not allowed to conduct independent practice or work in a facility without a licensed counselor on the premises. Carefully review your state statutes on this issue to clarify supervision requirements.

Seek a dedicated Christian counselor with a reputation for excellence in experience, education, and ethics to be your clinical supervisor. Your counseling center will thrive under responsible teaching and encouragement. Licensed Christian professionals with longstanding careers agree that regular peer consultation with fellow Christian practitioners helps them avoid becoming stagnant in their counseling approaches.

Supervision can be part of the job description for a qualified staff member, or a contract supervisor can be paid a retainer fee or an hourly fee for the actual consultation time provided. The fee for consultation or supervision is usually the same amount that the supervisor charges for a counseling hour.

Professional Groups

Competent pastoral and professional counselors are lifelong learners. A cost-effective way to enhance your counselor training is through continuing education programs. Local, regional, and national organizations abound with conferences, speakers, and workshops on a variety of general or specific counseling techniques. You may already hold membership in one or more national organizations such as the American Association of Christian Counselors or the Christian Association for Psychological Studies. Attending national conferences is a great opportunity to update your knowledge and interact with other Christian counselors.

You also need a local counselors group with whom you can participate on a regular basis. In addition to continuing education, these groups provide opportunities for you to network with potential referral sources, learn of specialty services, and form an effective lobby on counselor license legislation. Some Christian counselors are members of study groups that focus on special areas of psychotherapy from a purely professional approach. In many cities there are local affiliates of national counselor organizations that are slanted toward humanist and alternative lifestyle issues. You can get some useful information on professional issues and state or local issues related to counseling from the secular organizations if no Christian professional alternative is available. However, attending such a meeting will clearly illustrate how little a believer can have in common with an unbeliever (2 Cor. 6:15).

In counseling, as in our Christian walk, we need the fellowship of believers! Depending on what is available in your community, you might want to start a local counselors fellowship to provide continuing education that is biblically based and professionally credible. Send out a call through local Christian radio and television stations and in the major newspaper's club notices inviting pastors and other church-linked ministries to join the group. In every city there is a potential core group of Christian counselors who hunger for this fellowship. Remember, you must continue to grow and develop your counseling skills if your ministry is to fulfill its mission.

Billing Service

Like many service professionals, counselors are reluctant to act as collection agents. Some of you will admit to feeling uncomfortable just asking the client for the fee at the end of each session. If that seems tough, imagine what it would be like to enter the lion's den of third-party reimbursement! Also, even anticipated payments from insurance carriers or managed-care organizations can be time consuming and complicated to collect. And all of these collections can be further hampered if you do not have electronic billing capability. If insurance billing accounts for more than 20 percent of your practice income, seriously evaluate the merits of in-house billing (manual or computer) versus a billing service.

Do-it-yourself billing, alone or with the help of a secretary, requires dealing with precertifications, calling to verify outpatient mental health coverage, preparing claim forms, monitoring payments, and keeping an aging accounts list. You would need to add to this the cost of telephone time in tracking unpaid claims. In reality, the payment received is actually reduced by the hourly rate of the secretary's (or therapist's) time spent trying to collect the fees. Because of the added expenses involved in collection, some sole practitioner's refuse to accept any insurance assignments. Buying your own computer billing software may seem, on the surface, to speed up the process, however, the computer cannot take the place of a person when it comes to following up on outstanding claims. Even with computerized in-house billing, you or your secretary may have to spend hours of valuable time tracking insurance claims.

So before you make a final decision on insurance billing, consult with at least two experienced medical billing services. Look over their procedures and sample reports and be certain the service can handle electronic billing for all insurance companies and government claims. Medical billing specialist Lorna Yates devised the following checklist to help determine readiness and resources for doing the billing from your office versus contracting for full- service billing.

Expense or Services Needed for Electronic Billing

- Can you afford the initial capital expense for a computer, modem, and software?

- Do you know how to answer client and insurance company inquiries?

- How will you keep up with changes in legislative and regulatory issues?

- What is the frequency of processing claims: daily, weekly, bimonthly?

- Who will train your staff person in data entry, posting, and insurance coding?

- What are the estimated additional costs of computer forms and supplies?

- Can your computer and software be upgraded for expanded volume or to comply with rule changes (i.e., Medicare claims procedures)?[2]

If this list seems intimidating and too costly for your practice, consider a short-term contract (annually renewable) with a billing service. Expect to pay 7 to 9 percent of gross collections. Compared with the added salary for a secretary with billing experience, plus forms, office time, long-distance calls and collections, a billing service can be a bargain. Also, a billing service that charges on gross collections (not on the amount billed) does not get paid until you get paid—clearly a win-win situation.

MARKETING CONSULTANT

During the start-up phase and at periodic stages in your practice, a qualified marketing consultant can add the spark needed to attract more clients. By looking over your business plan and becoming familiar with your target client, a marketing consultant designs and implements strategies that complement your practice.

The affordable way for a new practice to hire marketing consultation is to request an initial review followed by project contracts. Marketing services are available from full-service advertising agencies that also have media, art, printing, and design departments. Although you will pay premium prices for this convenience, larger agencies do have top creative talent and good media contacts. However, you can probably negotiate more favorable terms with an independent marketing consultant. This specialist will recommend or arrange any printing, art, logo designers, and other services that are needed. The independent marketing consultant is available on an hourly rate or for a fee per job. If you are totally intimidated by marketing, at least get some help to begin your practice. But before turning all your marketing over to an outsider, consider that no one can convey your sense of dedication and ministry as well as you can.

STAFFING YOUR PRACTICE

SECRETARIAL EMPLOYEES

Having skilled support staff can compound income in a growing or group practice. Unfortunately the obvious (salary) and obscured (taxes and benefits) costs of hiring a secretary for a new practice are often beyond the budget. As an employer, you foot the bill for base salary, FICA, FUTA, and worker's compensation.[3.] Depending on your state, these mandated costs can add 10 to 15 percent to the total salary expense. You will also have to pay double wages for any days that a temporary worker is brought in to fill the regular secretary's vacation or sick-leave days.

More and more government regulations increase the per employee cost for small businesses. Beyond those concerns, small businesses are less able to afford medical insurance, retirement plans, and other benefits that attract experienced employees. A new practice that offers only minimum wage, no benefits, and a limited opportunity for advancement may have to work up to justifying a full-time secretarial employee.

There are four affordable substitutes to a full-time secretary-receptionist for sole practitioners and smaller counseling centers.

1. Arrange for a twenty-four-hour answering service with calls transmitted to an alphanumeric pager. This type of pager has a small screen on which a phone number or message can be displayed. A real advantage of the alphanumeric pager is that its mini-screen shows full messages such as, "Ms. Smith needs to reschedule 4 P.M. appointment" or "Mr. Jones in crisis—call immediately." This pager requires a telephone line that is placed on call-forward to the answering service. Consult your local telephone company for the availability of call forwarding services in your area. You can still call out on that line or remove forwarding and answer incoming calls. Whether you are in a counseling session or stuck in traffic, you will never be out of touch with your clients or with your office. And clients usually feel that talking with a private answering service is more personal and comforting than leaving a message on an answering machine. For less than $100 per month (for twenty-four-hour service plus pager), my clients can locate me anytime within a five-county area. If several counselors in your center share the answering service fee and carry individual pagers, the per person cost may be as low as $40 each per month. You can't get a secretary for those low prices. And a secretary could not always locate you outside of the office.

Less expensive pagers that function without an answering service greet the caller with a shrill tone and expect the caller to recognize that as the signal to enter a message or telephone number. However, if the client does not understand how or when to dial in their number, the counselor will probably miss a lot of important calls.

2. Another option is part-time office work performed by a contract worker. Secretarial services will lease such workers on an hourly or daily basis. The advantage to you is that you pay a flat rate and the worker remains an employee of the service instead of being your employee. If you are not satisfied with a worker, you can ask the secretarial service to send a different worker or request a certain worker with skills for a specific task. With leased workers, you do not have to hire, fire, train, or negotiate benefits.

3. Part-time office work may also be done by a college student who works evenings or occasional day hours depending on his or her class schedule. A Christian student majoring in counseling will find this a double blessing: a paycheck plus exposure to the operational aspects of a counseling practice.

4. Part-time office work can also be handled by a physically challenged worker. In this situation, typing, mailing, or basic bookkeeping is done on a contract basis by a mobility-limited person from his or her home. It is possible to receive tax breaks for hiring disabled workers; ask your accountant to research the current tax rules. In any case, you are providing supplemental income for a worker who is usually well motivated and focused on the task.

PROFESSIONAL EMPLOYEES

Adding counselors as employees of your center involves the same issues of competitive pay and benefits as previously discussed for secretarial employees. The screening of associate counselors is even more critical to safeguard the quality and reputation of your practice. In church-linked centers, counselors may also be associate pastors and thus be employees of the church on loan to the center (or vice versa). Remember that the salary, benefits, and expenses of the counselor come from the budget of the employer. Licensed counselors command a higher salary or fee split and benefits than unlicensed counselors. Counselor-associates generally expect that the practice will do the marketing and deliver the clients to their office doors. On the other hand, if you have some overflow of clients but want the associate to do his or her own prospecting, make this clear in the original agreement.

Many start-up practices bring in counselors under an informal association or tenants agreement, as discussed in chapter 3. Whether you have control (as with employees) or affiliation (as with tenants), be certain that all counselors agree to practice in one accord with the center's mission statement and ethical standards.

NOTES

1. CFP and Certified Financial Planner are federally registered service marks of the International Board of Standards and Practices for Certified Financial Planners (IBCFP), Denver, Colorado. ChFC is a designation offered by the American College, Bryn Mawr, Pennsylvania.

2. Lorna Yates, *Medical Billing: Which System Is Best for You?* (Tampa: Healthcare Billing Services, 1991).

3. FICA is the Federal Insurance Compensation Act, and FUTA is the Federal Unemployment Tax Act, see chapter 9.

Chapter Six

How to Maximize Marketing Impact with Minimal Cost

Ask and it will be given to you; seek and you will find; knock and the door will be opened to you.

Luke 11:9

MARKETING IS A HARMONIOUS BLEND of planning and vision. These elements are interdependent cornerstones on which the long-range success of your practice is built. The initial objective of a marketing plan is to inform potential clients of your services. And those clients can't beat a path to your door if they don't know where your office is located! An ongoing marketing effort reflects the type, tone, and professionalism of your counseling practice.

Winning marketing strategies adhere to the seven Cs of Communication:

1. Credibility: This factor is built on your performance and your clients' respect for your competence as a practitioner.

2. Context: Communication must be reality-based to confirm rather than contradict your message.

3. Content: Your message must have meaning and uphold the value system of the receiver.

4. Clarity: The farther a message must travel, the simpler it must be.

5. Continuity and Consistency: Repeat the basic message to create awareness.

6. Channels: Use established communication channels that are respected by your target clients.

7. Capability of Audience: Make sure your communication is geared to the level of the person who receives it.[1]

Each time you consider a new marketing approach, carefully evaluate it along these professional public relations criteria. Marketing professionals will tell you that starting a promotional plan without careful testing of the message and delivery system gives new meaning to the old adage "haste makes waste."

Can your counseling center become known in your area without a big-budget advertising campaign? Yes! The basic approaches are to gain media recognition and sound your own trumpet. The ideas that follow are low-budget but have the potential for a high rate of return.

Gaining Media Recognition

Press Releases

Sending out press releases is a time-honored method of attracting media attention for your programs or newsworthy events. An effective press release tells the who, what, when, where, why, and how in a brief, neat format (see sample in Appendix E). The universal rule is to write tight. You must capture a busy editor's attention quickly or your *news* will hit the wastebasket. To do so, you have to state your case on one page with crisp writing, accurate information, and plenty of white space, (ample margins surrounding your copy where editors can write in editing or typesetting instructions).

Take time to slant or direct your release to the size and audience of each publication. Just a slight rewrite or additional copy can tailor your release to each audience; short, attention-grabbing copy for sophisticated media; an expanded version for less selective community media; personalized text for hometown media; and technical information for counseling and pastoral media.[2] Print your release on good quality white paper—avoid pastel or neon colors. You can use the news release template from a computer program or you can purchase laser printer or copier paper with a press release headline. Either the template or purchased headline paper is acceptable as long as there is plenty of room for your information and there are no cute graphics. Select a type style that's easy to read even with bold or italics and never use odd typefaces or computerized cursive. Type your press release double-spaced with wide margins and do not neglect to proofread it carefully. Your word processor's spelling checker will not catch all errors, such as *there* instead of *their*. If the spelling is careless why would an editor be impressed with your news or achievements?

Just as one man's trash is another man's treasure, so a city editor's trash basket is filled with advertising that is poorly disguised as a press release. Editors are gatekeepers who must filter out the trivial and pursue the news of interest to their readers. Some newsworthy events in your counseling center could be:

• The addition of services that are needed in your community.

• Expanding or moving your office.

• A community or professional presentation by a noted guest speaker.

• Significant research you presented at a conference.

• Your statement of client advocacy relating to underserved mental health needs in the community.

• Debuting a special event or project to benefit the community.

• Announcing a link between your counseling center and a regional or national group that enhances your services.

As a rule of thumb, news value is based on timeliness, proximity to the community, prominence of people and events, unusualness or departure from the norm, human-interest factors, and conflict between people or philosophies.[3] Many local newspapers also have designated sections for business news and community calendars. Address these releases to the editor of the appropriate section. This provides additional opportunities to receive free publicity for information that is not hard news such as your parenting seminar, expanded Saturday counseling hours, recognition of an award, and promotion or addition of staff.

If the newspaper or magazine accepts photos with press releases, include a black-and-white, portrait-style photo of the person featured in the release. Color photos may not be accepted, and if they are, the photo quality may suffer when printed in black and white. If the photo you want to send is of a group of people or is an exterior shot, discuss it with the editor. If a publication does accept your photo, limit the group of individuals in the photo to four or less because larger group shots are often discarded due to the copy space required to identify each person. Print or type the names of each person pictured on a plain label, indicating left-to-right or front-to-back order in row 1, row 2, etc. Affix the label to the lower section of the photo. (Using a label prevents making pen marks that can damage the photo.) Some newspapers keep photos of community business and professional leaders on file while others discard these after each use. You will have to find out the policy of each publication. But never assume the photo you sent last year is still on file. Since photo reprints are inexpensive, why not keep a supply handy. For the sake of quality and composition, most newspapers prefer to have their photographers take action shots.

INTERVIEWS AND COMMENTS

Local media value their list of practitioners who are willing to give a brief interview on a topic or news event related to their area of expertise. Due to the timeliness of on-the-spot news coverage, radio and television news programs compete for stories that are still unfolding. Hence the *sound bite*, or targeted comment, from a specialist on an issue that is pertinent to his or her field adds to the credibility of the report. You can become a media resource within your counseling specialty. For example, if you have experience working with spouse abuse, you may be called to comment on a local domestic violence story. Or your counseling center's approach to working with homeless families, from counseling to case management, could make a good human-interest feature story for a noon news show or public affairs program.

Generally, it is up to you to make yourself known to local media. A useful tool of introduction is a media kit that consists of: (1) a brochure or a summary of your counseling services, (2) biographies and photos of the counselors, (3) a schedule of upcoming groups and seminars, and (4) a copy of your newsletter or an article you have written. Each page must be neatly typed, grammatically correct, and printed on letterhead or high-quality paper. Package these items inside an attractive two pocket folder with a business card inserted in a slot or neatly stapled to the outside of the pocket. Deliver a media kit personally to the city editor and business editor at each newspaper and to assignment editors at radio and television stations that cover your city news. In some rural areas, the primary media headquarters may come from a larger city nearby. In that case you will want to visit both the headquarters and any local offices.

Establishing rapport is the first step to selling yourself as someone worth interviewing. What earns repeat opportunities to be quoted in local media is dependability. It goes without saying that a reporter working on a tight deadline does not have time for you to research your response and call back tomorrow. Of course, that does not mean you can fake a response or give a flip answer. When you do not have the information or expertise to comment, simply say so honestly and recommend another counselor who does. Questions that are within your expertise need to be answered with nontechnical language in short sentences, while remaining within the bounds of confidentiality, law, and ethics. If you are unskilled at extemporaneous speaking or visibly uncomfortable in pressure situations, decline an on-the-spot interview. Waffling only irritates newspaper reporters and is embarrassingly obvious during a broadcast. Instead, find another spokesperson for your counseling center or limit your public speaking to more controlled situations, such as seminars and prepared statements.

Support Groups

An effective ministry for those gifted in helping others (1 Cor. 12:28) is in organizing support groups that expand on and provide a transition from the work done in counseling. Thus, many counseling centers offer support groups as both a service to clients and as a community outreach. Newspapers and some broadcast media present regular updates on support groups as a public service.

Before starting a support group, check for a related national group that may provide valuable information on existing groups in your area, new group planning, programs, resources, and prospective member referrals. This approach has proven effective in my work with such groups as Adoptive Families of America, Parenting Within Reason, and Alzheimer's Disease and Related Disorders Association. *The Self-Help Sourcebook*[4] lists a wide variety of support groups and gives practical tips on how to form a group.

JOINT VENTURES WITH LOCAL CHURCHES OR OTHER COUNSELORS

Combining the talents and resources of several Christian counselors in private and church-linked practices can produce a special program that commands media attention. The quick road to recognition is to bring in a well-known author as the featured speaker for a conference or as the sole speaker for an evening program. Give the author's publisher plenty of information on local talk shows and newspaper interview opportunities and encourage the publisher to send a book and press kit to each one. Such efforts pay off in additional free publicity for your program every time the speaker is interviewed by local media. If you invite reporters to attend the event, arrange a quiet room for mini press conferences and broadcast interviews.

Apply the same enthusiastic promotion approach if your program committee decides to feature local counselors. Send out media kits about the conference with speaker bios, a program schedule, and a brief (two-to-three-paragraph) statement from each speaker with quotable highlights of his or her presentation. Too often we fail to recognize the talents of local counselors. If you have been unaware of their achievements, chances are the local media does not know about them either. A special community program and highly qualified local counselors are the ingredients for a human-interest story with a local-counselor-makes-good emphasis.

LETTERS TO THE EDITOR

Newspapers provide an open forum to readers through letters to the editor, guest editorials, and other reader-response columns. Why not take advantage of these opportunities to be the salt of the earth (Matt. 5:13) in print? For example, our regional newspaper printed my letter chastising the editor for running a comic strip with a demeaning remark about adoption. The letter described the comic's emotional impact on adopted children and noted the lack of sensitivity by a newspaper that usually prides itself on being unoffensive to any group. Identifying myself as an adoptive parent and an adoption-triad counselor added credibility to my comments. Although my phone number was not included, two new clients located me for counseling related to adoption issues because they agreed with my concerns on that subject.

Be selective about the issues to which you respond, and when you do respond, challenge without being rude or vitriolic. Let your letter display your expertise in identifying problems and offering constructive alternatives. This opportunity to express your viewpoint is a privilege within a free press system; it should not be overused or subtly commercialized.

GUEST COLUMNIST

Community newspapers and special interest papers (i.e., shoppers, minority newspapers, and newcomer-welcoming publications) are most receptive to a guest column on counseling issues. Before you meet with the editor, critically review other columns printed in that paper. Take note of the style, tone, length, and focus. What do the writing, events coverage, and advertising tell you about the reader demographics of the publication? Is your target client found among the readers of this newspaper? If not, your column will not serve as an outlet for educating the public and promoting your services, it will merely serve as ego gratification. Furthermore, you can be sure that a sharp editor will be as concerned as you are that your practice and expertise match the readers' profile.

Again, dependability is crucial. You must be able to meet deadlines, rewrite as requested, and submit your masterpiece to merciless editing. Editors are looking for columns that present fresh and relevant material. You can write that column. But bear in mind that such publicity opportunities are not totally free. Although you do not pay for the space directly, you do pay with your time and efforts to research and produce each column.

Sounding Your Own Trumpet

Newsletters

Thanks to advanced word-processing programs, laser printers, and discount copiers, the locally produced newsletter is feasible for even small counseling practices. Newsletters can accomplish several goals: they can educate clients on special topics, announce upcoming events, highlight new services, introduce staff (photos and bios), and create an image of professionalism and credibility.

If you are not print-savvy, hire a marketing consultant to design the newsletter format and assist with the first production. Begin simply by using an 8 1/2 x 11 inch single page printed on both sides. Choose a subtle color of paper, black ink, and two or three columns of copy. As you become proficient at writing crisp copy and making uncluttered layouts you may want to expand to four pages.

Although you may not realize it, local print shops are a valuable resource of clip art, typesetting ideas, and constructive critiques for do-it-yourself newsletter editors. While desktop publishing on your office computer is even less expensive, it lacks the advantage of a professional printer's expertise. Another helpful resource is word-processing programs that contain preset newsletter formats complete with a masthead that you can customize. For additional details on color choices, paper stock, type styles, and headlines, consult books on printing and desktop publishing.

If you want to gather newsletter ideas, become a newsletter collector. Start a file of newsletters from any source that illustrates "the good, the bad and the ugly." You will quickly find some of each! In looking critically through these samples, notice the different formats that are used to present the feature story and take heed of tacky mistakes in arranging graphics that you will want to avoid. In summary, the keys to an effective newsletter are (1) quality information, (2) easy reading, (3) word pictures that capture the interest of the reader, and (4) consistency of publication.

BROCHURES FOR YOUR PRACTICE

The brochure is an expected introduction to a professional practice. It answers the essential inquiries of who you are, what services you provide, when the office is open, where it is located, why you are in practice (mission statement), and how you are qualified (degree, license, ordination) to provide counseling.

Additional brochures can be developed for special programs. For example, my Pre-Adoption Parenting Group brochure (reproduced on pages 84–85) serves as an introduction, topic outline, annual calendar of group dates, and mini promotion of my adoption workbooks. The third panel is a tear-away registration form with space on the back side for registrants to list friends (prospects!) who are interested in adoptive parenting. The entire brochure is composed on my computer using AmiPro software[5] and a laser printer, then it is copied inexpensively at a print shop.

You will find more excellent suggestions on writing and designing a brochure in Elizabeth Adler's book, *Print That Works*. Adler gives a simple diagram showing which panel gets read first and what type of information is best placed on each panel.[6] Her approach is similar to what I learned years ago in preparing broadcast promotional brochures. Here's how brochures for my counseling practice are arranged on an easy-to-print three-fold brochure:

The *program brochure* promotes a specific program or event (see Table 6.1). The same format can be used for a *product brochure* that presents books, tapes, or other counseling related resources.

Table 6.1
Program or Product Brochure Format

Inside the Open Brochure

	Panel 1	Panel 2	Panel 3
Program/ Product:	introduction; goals/ objectives	program elements; program schedule	registration/ order form or information request

If you are considering Adoption
or
you are awaiting the birth of your child, this is the time to prepare to become Adoptive Parents.

Pre-Adoption Parenting Group is like a "lamaze for adoption" in which you become aware and sensitive to the major issues of adoption.

Trends of Adoption in the 90's include

** greater openness in the process

** communication by letters or meeting with your child's Birthgiver

** more information shared on the child's medical and genetic heritage

** emphasis on counseling for the Birthgiver & Birthpartner to make a healthy resolution of the decision

** early introduction of the adoptive story to enhance your child's sense of belonging, security and love.

Pre-Adoption Parenting Group prepares you to understand and obtain the greatest benfits from these new Adoption trends.

Your Group leader is
Kathie Erwin, PhD, LMHC, NCC, adoptive parent of twins and experienced Adoption Triad Counselor.

Session I 9 am - 10:30 am

Adoption & Infertility Resolution
Preparing for the Homestudy
Open Placement vs. Open Adoption
Labor Pains of Adoption (delays & fears)

Session II 10:45am - 12:30pm

Telling the Adoption Story
Transcultural/Transracial Adjustments
Dealing with Dual Heritage
Developmental Stages & Adoption Issues

Groups are held at Medfield Hospital, 12891 Seminole Blvd, Largo, Fl. on these Saturdays in 1993:

January 16   March 20   May 22
August 21   October 16

$50 per couple for Sessions I & II
$30 per couple for Session II (if you have completed adoption placement)

For further information, call Dr. Erwin, 585-6010. Pre-paid registrations will be confirmed by mail.

To register for **Pre-Adoption Parenting Group** complete this section, tear off and mail with a check for $50 payable to Dr. Kathie Erwin.

__Jan 16 __Mar 20 __May 22
__Aug 21 __Oct 16

Name _____

Name _____

Address _____

City _____ ST ___ ZIP ___

Work # _____ Home # ___

Have you tried adoption before? __yes __no
If yes, what was the result? _____

Have you selected a placement source?__yes __no
Attorney _____ Agency _____

Are you involved in contact with Birthgiver?
What method: letters__ telephone__ meeting__

On what aspect of Adoption and Adoptive Parenting do you feel that you have the least understanding or need more information?
_____

* Singles are encouraged to bring their support person or future grandparent at couples rate.

Pre-Adoption Parenting Group

Your first step toward understanding the processes, emotions and parenting issues of Adoption.

Kathie Erwin, PhD, LMHC
Adoption Triad Counselor

Introducing your Group leader....

Kathie Erwin, Ph.D., is a Clinical Psychotherapist, Licensed Mental Health Counselor and National Certified Counselor in private practice in Clearwater, Florida.

Her interest in Adoption comes both from personal experience and work as an Adoption Triad Counselor.

An infertility alumna, Dr. Erwin is now the proud mother of twin girls, through the miracle of adoption.

This Pre-Adoption Parenting Group is taken from the full text of Dr. Erwin's Pre/Post Adoption Adjustment Counseling Model for Birthgivers and Adoptive Parents, which is devoted to "nurturing triad relationships". She is the author of **A Special Plan,** Birthgiver's workbook and **A Special Blessing,** Adoptive Parent's workbook.

...and now a word from the twins;

Kelly: Adoption is a great way to become a REAL family.

Robin: Adoption proves that God really loves all the children of the world.

REGISTER NOW!

to reserve your place for the

Pre-Adoption Parenting Group

date of your choice!

Invite Friends or Colleagues who are interested in Adoption. This brochure will be mailed to them:

name _____

address _____

city _____ st ____ zip _____

name _____

address _____

city _____ st ____ zip _____

Outside Areas on Folded Brochure

	Panel 4	Panel 5	Panel 6
program/ product:	prospect request; other materials for sale	speaker's bio; endorsements	cover: simple, clean logo, art, graphics, and photo

I save money on program brochures and added mailing costs by including an annual calendar of dates and locations for repeated events. This requires advance planning but results in less work. Another idea is to add items that tease the readers' interest such as titles of upcoming programs. Brochures that promote books, tapes, or courses can be more general and used with a cover letter or changed to a self-mail format.

The *generic* or *institutional brochure* includes practical, undated information that will help the potential client decide if this is the type of services desired (see Table 6.2). This suggested arrangement is similar to the previous example with some changes for copy.

Table 6.2
Bridgework Generic Brochure Format

Inside the Open brochure

	Panel 1	Panel 2	Panel 3
generic/mailer:	introduction; mission statement	services; types of clients served	call to action; phone, hours, map

Outside Areas on Folded Brochure

	Panel 4	Panel 5	Panel 6
generic/mailer:	brief staff résumés; special programs	return address in left corner; printed bulk- mail permit	cover: simple and clean logo, art, or graphics

Folded in thirds, the generic brochure can be mailed alone or stuffed in a no. 10 business envelope (see the sample brochure on pages 88–89).

Whatever the purpose of your brochure, start with a simple design and low production costs. Why? With experience you will find that the test of time and results is the best feedback. That means that no matter how carefully you consider all the elements, you will come up with corrections or additions for the next run. However, if your garage is piled high with expensive, slick, multicolor brochures that you can't bear to waste you will feel locked into an inferior product.

BROCHURES ON ISSUES

Another helpful idea is to create a series of brochures that deal with treatment options and the biblical approach to current psychosocial problems. For example, you might develop a series that features a variety of topics such as "A Christian Counselor's Response to Depression." By simply changing the copy and the title you can focus on other counseling issues such as parenting, addiction, grief, infertility, pain, anxiety, or any other topic relevant to your target client. It is a good idea to retain the same brochure format so it is easily identifiable as part of the series. Place your photo or a photo of your office on the back middle section (of a three-fold brochure) with information about services, hours of operation, phone number, and a map to your office.

Distribute these brochures free to physicians, dentists, chiropractors, attorneys, and funeral directors for use in their waiting rooms. If your budget permits, also provide a clear-plastic freestanding rack so your brochures are not scattered or lost in piles of magazines. Another inexpensive way to get these brochures distributed is to pay a teenager to pin brochures to bulletin boards at apartment complexes, laundromats, grocery stores, public libraries, bowling alleys, and bus stops. However, where necessary, always get permission from the owner or manager before leaving the brochures.

EDUCATIONAL WORKSHOPS

Family issues, relationships, and self-improvement are hot-selling topics today. Just scan a magazine rack at the local bookstore to see how many lead articles fit in these categories. You can become an important teaching resource in your community by providing regular educational workshops on these

Our Counseling Center is a unique place of healing and growth. The focus is a well-rounded approach to a person's suffering, which includes the emotional, physical and spiritual aspects of victimization.

COUNSELING UNIT

Our Counsel unit provides both individual and group counseling. The individual counseling sessions allow the supervisor to focus on the personal and specific issues of their trauma. The group counseling helps a survivor connect with others, to receive feed-back and to understand their victimization in a larger sense.

OUR COUNSELING UNIT PROVIDES GROUP EXPERIENCES IN THE FOLLOWING AREAS OF TRAUMA:

- Women's incest Group
- Men's incest Group
- Dysfunctional Family Group
- Eating Disorder Group
- Women's Issues Group
- Multiple Personality Disorder Group
- Family/Friends of Multiple Personality Disorder
- Children's Self-esteem Group
- Parenting Group

INDIVIDUAL COUNSELING ISSUES CAN INCLUDE:

- All Aspects of Abuse
- Personality Disorders
- Post Traumatic Stress
- Family Issues
- Spirituality
- Anger
- Sexuality

Educational Unit

Our Educational Unit provides training to counselors, clergy and other care-givers in the area of Victimology, based on our national clinical book, _Counseling Victims of Violence._ These tailor-made workshops have been taught at the undergraduate and graduate levels....also at national conferences such as the American Association for Counseling and Development, and the World Congress on Christian Counseling.

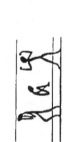

Workshops can be booked by calling our office:
(813) 530–4199

BRIDGEWORK MINISTRIES COUNSELING CENTER

(813) 530-4199

Bay Park Executive Center
18840 Hwy. U.S. 19 North #450
Clearwater, Florida 34624

BRIDGEWORK
MINISTRIES, INC.

Bay Park Executive Center
18840 Hwy U.S. 19 North #450
Clearwater, Florida 34624

PLACE
STAMP
HERE

Expressive Therapies

.....also offered through our Center is Expressive Therapies, which allows for a deeper expression of pain and healing. These week-end experiences have included:

- Art Therapy
- Wilderness Retreats
- Ropes Course
- Spiritual Inner Healing and Renewal

(Reprinted with permission of the Rev. Sandra Brown, director of Bridgework Ministries)

lifestyle issues. Initially these workshops serve as prospecting opportunities whereby potential clients or referral sources have the opportunity to observe you in action and form impressions about your expertise and communication style. Offer workshops at no charge, but ask participants to preregister due to limited space. This will also help you to prepare adequate handouts and provide comfortable seating. After you build a reputation for presenting quality workshops, you can consider charging a small fee. But remember that potential clients are not as likely to pay big bucks for a few hours of teaching when they can buy a self-help book for twelve to fifteen dollars. Don't price yourself out of your own market!

Many counselors prefer to hold workshops at their offices or at a church so that participants become aware of and comfortable in the counseling center. However, while an audience of current clients, church members, or other Christians will attend at either your office or church, these locations may prove too imposing for some prospective clients, including those who rarely attend church. If you hold your workshop at other community locations you enable a new potential audience to learn of your services in a less threatening environment. Good choices for free or low-cost meeting space include the public library, a mall's community room, city recreation centers, a classroom or gym at a Christian school, university or hospital lecture halls, and civic club buildings. In these instances you will want to be aware of any restrictions and implications of association in using a secular business conference center, public school, city hall, or any facility where events that are antagonistic to the Christian lifestyle are frequently held. For example, if the meeting room you select hosts an abortion rights rally in the morning and your seminar in the evening, you will risk guilt-by-association.

Promote your workshop with a variety of low-cost, high-visibility methods such as press releases, notices in the newspaper's community calendar, flyers posted in local businesses, posters in local Christian bookstores, and bulletin inserts distributed at churches within your target market. You might also consider asking a Christian business owner to stuff your announcement with his or her company's monthly statements. Mail stuffers that are one-third of an 8 1/2 x 11 inch sheet of paper require no extra postage and insert without folding. If the topic is family or parenting, ask principals of local Christian schools to announce your workshop at the next parent-teacher meeting. When you send bulletin inserts or flyers to other churches be sure to include a personalized letter to each pastor describing the focus and biblical basis of your program as well as a summary of your training or expertise. These are all inexpensive ways to reach an interested population within your target market; your only cost is for paper, copies, and some postage.

Special Events

Many counseling centers offer special programs for the community based on designated events such as National Mental Health Month (May), Family Day (in August) and National Singles Week (in September).[7] In my area, several professional counseling centers offer free depression screenings during National Mental Health Month. Look for ways to bring a local emphasis to these larger campaigns. This might include obtaining generic brochures and other resources from the national sponsor to use in your local program.

If you do not find a national day that reflects your interests, create your own event. Your counseling office can sponsor a Community Mental Health Awareness Day at your church or in a mall. Invite private, church-linked, and government services to make presentations and to staff information booths at the event. Or you may choose to eliminate the secular resources and plan a Christian Wellness Fair featuring only Christian family and mental health services.

Be a Guest on TV, Radio, or Cable Public Service Shows

Information in your media kit or your community workshops may attract the attention of local broadcasters looking for a new slant on a story with a broad appeal. Once again those ever-popular topics of family issues, relationships, and self-improvement are tailor-made for an articulate counselor. Look and listen to several locally produced radio and TV public service programs. Notice how each guest conveys a message. What was the nonverbal message given by each guest? Was it congruent with the verbal message or image that he or she attempted to convey? Why are some counselors interviewed frequently on local TV? The answer is simple: They appear comfortable on camera; they have the ability to present complex issues in lay terms; they share useful ideas; and they display a rapport with both the interviewer and the unseen television audience. Of course, it is more challenging to communicate in an interesting and believable manner on radio. You need to be animated without sounding fake and intense about your topic without seeming fanatic. Clearly, you must understand the performance aspects of radio and television. Popular talk-show guests are not the ones with the most degrees, but those with the most media-ease.

Radio and television leave strong impressions that can help or harm your public image. That is why research and practice are vital before you consider this source of promotion. To begin this process you might want to hire a work-at-home parent or a physically challenged homebound adult as your "media monitor." Over a period of four to eight weeks, this individual can identify, watch, and report on local radio, and TV shows that use local guests. The information gathered should track the types of shows (public affairs, education, call-in, and morning or noon news) and the target audience (general, women, parents, teens, etc.) of a specified media. As you analyze the information that has been gathered, select the shows that display the most interest in counseling issues and put these on your A list. Make a B list of shows on the periphery of counseling that could use your expertise if it were slanted to meet a special interest. For example, on a minority-issues forum aired on public affairs television you might talk about the emotional stresses of multicultural urban living.

Once you have categorized programs into these two lists, ask your media monitor to telephone every show on the A list to find out these important facts: (1) the name of the producer or interviewer who books guests; (2) how far in advance guests are booked; (3) if you can present your book, brochure, or workshop information during the interview; and (4) whether guests are interviewed live or prerecorded. Record this information in a card file or a computer file and update it at least twice a year.

Appearing on television is both exciting and intimidating. We have all seen interviews where the guest looked frightened and fidgety or spoke in an unappealing singsong voice. It is human nature in these situations to be so distracted by the method of presentation that we lose focus on what is being said. Don't let this happen to you. Instead, practice for a media appearance by role-playing the interview with another counselor. Turn on every bright light in the room, sit in chairs facing each other, adhere to the typical time limitation, and have a staff member present as the observer. Keep your attention focused on the interviewer as you would in a one-on-one session with a client. Have the observer record every unattractive mannerism that will be accentuated by TV, such as fidgeting, slouching in the chair, frequent use of "you know" or "like," forced smiles, poor eye contact, rising voice tone when nervous, and long or rambling answers. Better still, tape the practice interviews with a video camera so you can review and critique your performance. Many first-timers cringe at the sight and sound of themselves being interviewed, but as a counselor you have an advantage for dealing with this response: Use your counseling skills to accept the disappointment as a learning experience. Once you have identified areas of weakness and potential drawbacks, practice how to make a better presentation. Then reframe your feelings of despair with excitement that this TV interview is the motivation to identify and change some habits that detract from your message in all areas of life.

Appearance is also an important part of conveying a message. Consider these tips on how to dress for success in a TV interview:

- Look professional but not stuffy, fashionable but not teenybopper trendy.
- Choose comfortable-fitting clothes: no tight collars that make your Adam's apple bulge or short skirts that restrict modest movement.
- Bright TV lights can raise temperatures on the set to more than 100 degrees, so skip the wools, sweaters, and heavy fabrics.

- Bold plaids, checks, and busy prints make even small people look like sick billboards.
- Avoid bright, white collars near your face; the glare is unattractive.
- Pastel collars or scarves near the neck soften and highlight your face.
- Subtle shades of blue, red, and blue-green look good; yellow, some greens, bright orange, and too much black are unappealing and overwhelming on camera.
- Men and women need lots of makeup just to look natural under studio lights.
- Wear small jewelry that does not clang, dangle, or reflect too much light.
- If you frequently look at your watch when nervous, don't wear it during the interview.

When you are doing a radio interview your voice and how you speak are as important as what you are saying. To be an effective radio communicator:

- Modulate your voice, raising and lowering the pitch within a pleasant, conversational range.
- Take a brief pause to consider each question.
- Do not interrupt the interviewer; listeners are confused about who is talking unless the voices are very recognizable.
- Use vivid word pictures; listen to tapes of classic radio shows from the forties to hear the power of word choice and vocal expression in communicating what is not seen.
- Bring only a few papers or notecards; shuffling papers makes terrible noise and distracts the flow of an interview.
- Once you enter the studio avoid saying anything you don't want to be broadcast; you never know when the microphone is on and the tape running. Today's off-the-cuff comment can quickly become tomorrow's embarrassing local headline!

If you are interested in more tips for radio and TV appearances, look in your local library for books on public relations, broadcasting, and media interviews.

Another twist on the talk show is the *infomercial*, a slickly produced commercial that is filled with useful information as well as promotion for a service or product. Less glossy (and less expensive) versions of infomercials are available on local cable access channels and some talk radio stations. But before you sign a twenty-six-week contract for a commitment like this, which could obliterate your marketing budget, get a second opinion from a marketing consultant with broadcast experience. Smart marketing techniques will match your target audience to the show's audience demographics. Since the key to success in broadcast promotion is "reach and frequency," the marketing consultant will want to consider what extent of your target market can be reached by that show and will determine the need for repetition or frequency of delivering the message. Other important tests of efficiency include "cost per thousand" and "cost per gross rating point." An experienced broadcast sales representative can show you how these industry terms translate into measures of effectiveness in getting your message to the right audience.

Public Speaking

Program committees for local civic, church, community, and support groups toil under the task of finding interesting speakers for their meetings. Let them know you are the speaker they seek! You can find mailing addresses for most community organizations through lists or directories that are usually available at the public library or chamber of commerce. Another option is to scan the meeting notices in the newspaper community calendar. Clip out the notices and glue them onto file cards for easy reference. When you or your secretary telephone the person listed in a club notice, ask for the name and address of the speakers committee chairperson. Offer to send a media kit with a list of three or four topics you can present. Give a one-paragraph explanation of each proposed topic slanted toward the interests and demographics of the group.

For example, the same general information on stress management can be adapted for a business women's group (Overstressed for Success), Christian business owners group (Service and Ministry to Your High-Stressed Clients) or parents group (When You Have More Stress Than You Can Handle). When you are invited to speak to a local group, remember to bring your counseling center brochure or the counseling issues brochures as handouts. You might also want to create a handout for the audience that could include an outline of your presentation and other pertinent materials. Be sure to print your name, address, and office number on the handout and attach a business card. It is an opportunity for name recognition and referral that you do not want to miss.

Novice speakers are more likely to benefit more from on-the-podium experience, than reading about the techniques of effective public speaking. If you are interested in learning from other experienced speakers, you could contact a local branch of Toastmasters International,[8] an organization that teaches people how to express themselves before an audience. Its widely used methods of training and encouragement have transformed many shaky-handed, heart-racing neophytes into confident speakers. You might also want to consider taking courses on public speaking through a local college or adult education program. The truth of the matter is, giving a speech is like learning to hang glide: you have to risk falling to learn to soar.

Office Open House

The grand opening of your practice is an occasion to celebrate with an open house. Invite your church family, professional referral sources, community leaders, other Christian colleagues, and the local media. Prior to opening our first office, I decided that the occasion deserved something more significant than the worn out ribbon-cutting ceremony. Since the business was to be dedicated to the Lord in our hearts, it seemed fitting to do so in public. So we invited our pastor to officially open the office with Scripture readings and a blessing followed by praise songs. Because the opening ceremony was so unique it was covered in the community newspaper.

If you choose to have this type of office opening, do not hesitate to invite nonbelievers. Those who attend may ask important questions about the Lord as they talk with you about your new counseling services. One established professional who attended our office opening said he did not agree with "the religious thing" but he greatly respected our willingness to demonstrate our beliefs in this way.

You may choose to make the open house an annual event, marking the center's anniversary or celebrating the Christmas season. During the day offer several special programs or group sessions that your guests can visit. Although these sessions and other demonstrations will have to be staged, it is a good opportunity to introduce potentital clients to counseling procedures. Invite newcomers to sit in the group room and discuss how it feels to talk in a group or ask what they expect to happen in group counseling. Or you might adapt a format that's often used at conferences: the poster session. Station each counselor in a different room with a poster display and have him or her give an ongoing presentation of a counseling issue. With foresight and planning, the annual open house can serve both a social and teaching purpose.

The Strategic Evaluation Process

A procedure for regular checkups is necessary to find out if your marketing program is alive and well. Actually the analysis begins in the planning stages by distinguishing the two levels of marketing: first, master strategies that promote the overall mission and long-term objectives, and second, program strategies aimed at specific objectives or projects.[9] Marketing specialists often use a technique familiar to psychotherapists: the pre-test and post-test. Here are three essential strategic evaluation processes that even the do-it-yourself marketer can implement:

1. Pre-test the Message. It is easy to become so involved with the promotion piece you write that you overlook inconsistencies, jargon, or incomplete sentences. Give the copy to three people (not counselors) and ask them to retell the message in their own words. Was that what you intended to convey? If not, what incorrect message is being transmitted? Rework the copy, then retest it for comprehension.

You can add sophistication to your evaluation by borrowing a pre-test technique that is popular in market research: the focus group. Select two groups of ten people per group from your church and the community to serve as focus groups. Vary the demographics and socioeconomic representation within the group. For example, one focus group may contain a teenager, a working single mom, an unmarried single adult, a young married couple, an older married couple, a business man, a business woman, and a senior adult. If any of these people are not represented among your target clients, you may replace them with others more suitable. However, do not let your focus group become too limited or you risk slanting toward too much agreement—like the old fallacy of only "preaching to the choir." Present your marketing plan, brochure or advertisement to the focus groups and sit back to hear the responses. Your role is that of an observer and recorder of impressions; learn not just from what they say, but also from their facial expressions and tone of voice. The impressions you get from a well represented focus group reflect the current and experimental values of your community.[10] You do not want to let your focus groups become too complacent or too familiar because some of the less vocal members may become overwhelmed by the more assertive members. To avoid this problem, rotate membership in the focus group quarterly or semi-annually.

2. Rehearse Your Response. What if your TV appearance generates fifty calls to your office or a hundred requests to mail brochures? Can your office handle this demand promptly? Before you ask for a response, determine your ability to receive the results. This sounds simple, yet it is an often overlooked marketing problem.

Let's look at some simple solutions. If you appear on TV or radio at 11 A.M., be sure to have live telephone coverage at your office for the remainder of the workday, even during the lunch hour. Requests for brochures or other materials need to be filled in two to three working days so plan to have adequate printed materials and the proper size of envelopes available for mailing. For high demand, bring in teens or part-time helpers to fold and stuff. Whatever you offer to the public, be prepared to deliver it promptly before the interest and curiosity diminishes.

3. Post-test Impact Measures. If you look at marketing in an experimental psychology framework, marketing is the treatment and a post-test shows the results or changes in the target group. Retailers who run clearance sales and coupons can clearly count customer numbers and sales resulting from the marketing, but service providers are at a disadvantage in measuring marketing impact. The prospective client who calls for your brochure after hearing you on radio may not make a counseling appointment for six to twelve months. The response is not always immediate because the need may not be great at the time of the broadcast.

Counselors can test marketing benefit through quarterly evaluations of the quality and quantity of new clients and referrals. Qualitative statistics show how many new clients or referrals have the financial resources or types of problems that can be served in your center. Quantitative measures indicate the number of new clients, referrals, continuing clients, terminations, and dropouts. You can gather these statistics without revealing any confidential information. Under each of the quantitative categories of service use, describe clients with a simple code such as: M/35/D/300.02/R=church. That translates to: male, age thirty-five, divorced, 300.02 Generalized Anxiety Disorder, referred by your church. Caution: If you are not qualified under your state law to use DSM-III-R diagnostic criteria,[11] make another type of code for pastoral or lay counseling issues that are addressed.

A pattern of market segmentation is obtained by gleaning consumer and psychographic data from your recent cases. Consumer characteristics are demographic data such as age, sex, income, and residential location. Psychographic data reveal lifestyles, attitudes, and values.[12] These types of service analyses are less scientific, but they are highly useful for post-testing your marketing.

MARKETING AND MINISTRY

Just as Jesus instructed the disciples to go into the world and preach the gospel to all nations, so counselors have a mission to go into their communities and make known their services. Many lost people will not set foot in a church, and they slam the door on evangelistic teams. Yet those same people are crying out for help with their marriages, their children, and their personal pain. As we do good counseling and model the Christian walk, we are another arm of ministry. Can we responsibly fulfill the Great Commission in our workplace if we fail to attract our community, both believers and nonbelievers? As our marketing reflects our calling, marketing becomes ministry.

NOTES

1. Scott Cutlip and Allen Center, *Effective Public Relations,* 4th ed. (Englewood Cliffs, N.J.: Prentice Hall, 1971), 260–61. Reprinted by permission of Prentice-Hall, Englewood Cliffs, New Jersey.

2. Audrey Fisher, "Five Elements in Writing Successful Press Releases," *Writer's Digest,* May 1988.

3. Christine Friesleben Goff, *The Publicity Process,* 3d ed. (Ames, Iowa: Iowa State University Press, 1989).

4. Barbara White and Edward Madara, eds. *The Self-Help Sourcebook,* 4th ed. (Denville, N.J.: St. Clare's Riverside Medical Center, 1992). Ten dollars for first-class-mail delivery in the United States, fourteen dollars for overseas air mail.

5. AMIPRO 3.0 is a software program distributed by Lotus Development Corp., 1000 Abernathy Road, Atlanta, Georgia.

6. Elizabeth Adler, *Print That Works* (Palo Alto, Calif.: Bull Publishing Co., 1991).

7. *Chase's Annual Events; the Day to Day Directory of 1993* (Chicago: Contemporary Books, Inc., 1992).

8. Toastmasters International, P.O. Box 9052, Mission Viejo, California 92690-7052. Telephone 714-858-8255.

9. William Fallon, ed., *AMA Management Handbook,* 2d ed. (New York: AMACOM, 1983). Reprinted with permission of the publisher.

10. Judith Langer, "Focus Groups," *American Demographics,* February 1991.

11. *Diagnostic and Statistical Manual of Mental Disorders,* 3d ed., revised (Washington, D.C.: American Psychiatric Association, 1987).

12. Fallon, *AMA Management Handbook.* Used by permission.

Chapter Seven

Budgeting Your Finances and Your Time

Suppose one of you wants to build a tower. Will he not first sit down and estimate the cost to see if he has enough money to complete it?
Luke 14:28

Depending on your attitudes about money, you are likely to view a budget as either a straitjacket or a flight plan. If you are an impulse buyer who resists planning and has had no real experience with budgeting, then you probably think of a budget as a straitjacket. In contrast, if you are a wise steward of personal as well as business assets, you know that a budget is a flight plan that keeps you on course toward your goals. Within the managerial process, budgeting is "the orderly presentation of the anticipated results of a plan, project or strategy."[1] As part of your business plan and subsequent annual plans, you need to prepare a budget as a guide for ongoing operations.

Church-linked counseling centers operating as 501(c)(3) organizations are not profit-oriented; therefore, a different approach to budgeting is needed. A key issue for sliding-scale or low-fee counseling centers is that the cost of providing services often exceeds the fee income, which changes the definition of success as measured by for-profit centers. Supplemental operating funds are frequently obtained from donations, endowments, or fund-raising. In these situations, accounting expertise is required to determine the best reporting system, how to track program expenses within a budget, and whether to use multiple self-balancing fund accounts that allow donations to restricted or unrestricted accounts.[2] Nonprofit accounting must also withstand scrutiny from the state agency that regulates charitable solicitations, and the procedures must be sufficient for annual IRS reporting regulations. Budgeting for nonprofit organizations is much more complex than for a sole practitioner or a group private practice.

The actual format of your budget is not nearly as important as your commitment to operate within its parameters. This is especially crucial during the first year when you depend on projections without actual experience. Operating within the amount budgeted for that first year is the closest assurance you have that you can stay open for a second year. In subsequent years, budget adjustments can accommodate the growth and expansion of your counseling center. The following list of start-up costs can serve as the framework for a budget worksheet.

Start-up Costs

For most new businesses, expenses precede income. Those expenses are the start-up costs that are necessary for the business to become operational. Let's review the basic categories of expenses for a counseling practice. As you consider each category, make notes of your projected expenditures. When you have calculated your total projected start-up costs you may want to do some serious pruning of the shopping list. Remember that our God pledges to supply all of our needs, not all of our wants (Phil. 4:19). Without doubt a refusal to acknowledge the difference between needs and wants lies at the root of most business and personal financial failures. Although legitimate start-up costs are certainly needs, if your financial resources are limited, you will want to keep your beginning expenses lean and clean. These are sixteen basic start-up expenses:

1. OFFICE LEASE

While a church-linked counseling center is usually given space on the church premises, other counseling groups and private practice counselors will probably have to shop for rental office space in the community. Not only is a lease a serious legal obligation that needs to be reviewed by your attorney, it is also a major expense. Therefore, try to negotiate a short-term lease (one year) with renewable options. If the rental market in your city is overbuilt and underoccupied, you may be able to obtain rental space without a lease simply by paying the first plus last months' rental. You can also save monthly costs by leasing an existing office as it is, a condition that does not require modifications by the owner. With permission, you agree to paint, clean the carpets, and make minor changes. Regardless of the option that seems best to you, study the rental market in your city carefully before committing to a lease, or secure the services of a real estate agent who specializes in commercial rentals. (You will observe that office purchase is not discussed here. With no track record of practice and a low budget for start-up expenses, property purchase is really not a reasonable consideration at this beginning stage.)

2. FURNISHING

Make furnishing choices that complement your overall decorating plan for a comfortable, uncluttered, serene environment. Beware of buying unusual-shaped, custom-made, or large furnishings just to fit the first office because this will limit your options later if you move or just want to redecorate. A top priority is to have adequate, comfortable chairs in the reception room. For occasional overflow seating, stacking chairs used in the group room or kept in a storage closet can be pressed into service. Feel free to add your personal touches such as tasteful artwork, lush green or silk plants, soft lighting, and an interesting antique table.

Typically, a counselor's office appears as a mini living room with a relaxed, nonclinical atmosphere. If you must have a desk, keep it small and clean (or get a rolltop desk to cover the junk). Counselors who work in a group situation can add touches of their own personalities to the decor inside their offices. A suggestion might be to select chairs or a small sofa that can easily be recovered, or rotate a variety of colorful pillows and accessories. Flexible decorating can be inexpensive even while providing a periodic change of scenery for the counselor.

3. Moving

While new or used furnishings can be delivered by the store, this is not true for your personal file cabinet, the chairs from your attic, and the books piling up in your closet. The chore and cost of moving these items will be yours. The least expensive way to move is to rent a small moving truck and do it yourself. If that's not possible, look for a local mover who specializes in office or apartment moves. Generally these local movers are quite a bit less expensive than a national moving company. However, for your protection ask for a written estimate of costs and check the mover's replacement policy to cover breakage. A counseling group might hire one mover and split the costs, or each person can be responsible to pay the cost of moving his or her own items and then share the cost of moving reception room and secretarial furnishings.

4. Office Equipment

The well-planned electronic office pays for itself. A personal computer with word-processing and accounting programs, modem, fax machine (or fax board in your computer), and laser printer maximizes secretarial efficiency. However, you will probably need to prioritize these purchases to meet the growth demands of your practice. Few new practices can afford the full electronic office package in the beginning, so plan a system that is expandable.

Other office basics include locking file cabinets, a copy machine, a comfortable computer chair, and a secretarial desk or work station. Some equipment luxuries that may be added as the budget allows include a small refrigerator and microwave, an electronic postage scale, a TV with a video cassette playback unit, and an overhead projector (for use in teaching and community presentations).

5. THERAPEUTIC MATERIALS

This expense will vary depending on the type of counseling you provide. For example, a therapeutic playroom with dollhouse, building blocks, art supplies, and other items for play therapy are essential for counselors who work with children. If you are qualified to offer vocational, personality, or diagnostic testing, your office will need adequate supplies of test materials and some test kits.

If your practice is more generalized or you have not focused your practice yet, it is best to keep the initial materials purchased to a minimum. Also, in a group practice or office shared by several independent counselors, consider combining all your books into a shared-use internal library. As you become more expert in an area or fine tune your interests, you will be ready to make more useful purchases of books and other resources that contribute to your specialty.

6. PRINTING

A bare-bones printing package consists of letterhead stationery, envelopes, business cards, and a generic brochure. With a laser printer and multi-font program, you can avoid typesetting charges by preparing a camera-ready brochure and letterhead for a local print shop to produce. Or you can set up a letterhead template on which you type text and print the complete product from your laser printer on linen or high-quality paper. Print shops offer low-cost business envelopes and business cards with several layout options using black ink on white or cream stock. If you choose other colors of paper or ink, seriously evaluate the readability, extra costs, and psychological impact of the color choice.

7. ADVERTISING

The low-cost marketing strategies presented in chapter 6 are partly budgeted within the total advertising expenses. Other paid-advertising vehicles used by counselors are newspapers, radio, television, yellow pages, and bulletin sponsorships. Newspapers, radio, and TV have complex rate structures with the highest charges assigned for the most infrequent usage; the best rates are given for larger annual contracts. Other than community newspapers and smaller radio stations, new practices can rarely afford display or broadcast advertising. However, even cheap ads are too costly if they fail to reach your target market. A no-frills listing in the yellow pages counseling (or other) category is provided as part of your commercial phone-line charges. Larger, more colorful, and expensive yellow page ads are wasted unless you operate a crisis management center or offer free pastoral counseling to the public (if acceptable under your state laws). As for church and organizational bulletin ads, be very selective. Instead of the traditional business card ad, pay for a bulletin insert; a well-designed insert stands out and commands attention.

8. Telephone System

A one-person office is easily accommodated with a single phone line and an extension jack in the outer office; however, offices with more than three counselors or support staff will need a multi-station, expandable telephone system. There are systems that take messages, provide conference calls, serve as an intercom, and link with voice mail. The options are almost as out of sight as the prices. Add interest and finance charges to the purchase price and you quickly discover that purchasing a phone system can be a budget buster. Before you decide on a system, get estimates from your local phone company and at least two phone service competitors.

Many new practices find that a most cost-efficient choice is to lease a phone system or lease with an option to purchase. The leasing company will be happy to help you upgrade or expand your system at any time thus supplying continuity of service, repairs, and replacement. If you purchase a phone system that fails to meet your expansion needs, you will be stuck with monthly payments on obsolete, used equipment that may not even qualify for trade-in.

9. Supplemental Communication Systems

As all counselors know, counseling clients don't always schedule their crises during business hours. Thus, it is generally advisable to have additional ways to be contacted such as by pager, answering service, voice mail, or phone recorder. Compare the costs and effectiveness of each system for your workstyle and client base. A pager can be leased or purchased with a monthly fee for message transmissions, and if your practice uses more than three pagers, you can request a reduced fee for multiple units. Other choices include voice mail and phone recorders, which have become commonplace and (grudgingly) accepted for business use, and answering services, which offer more human warmth than their electronic counterparts. Whatever your budget allows, select at least one supplemental communication system.

10. PROFESSIONAL LICENSES AND FEES

A state-licensed mental health professional pays periodic fees for license renewal and the cost of continuing education necessary to maintain the license. Estimate at least $25 per credit hour multiplied by the minimum number of continuing-education hours required by your state licensing board. Also include any membership fees in local or national counselor organizations.

11. LOCAL OCCUPATIONAL LICENSES

Contact the city and county governments in which your office is located for rules about occupational licenses. If your office is in an unincorporated part of the county, only a county license may be necessary. Otherwise, expect to apply for and annually renew occupational licenses in both city and county. Even church-linked counseling centers that offer services to the public need to verify their status on occupational licensing with the appropriate governmental authorities.

12. INSURANCE

Because insurance is such a complex topic, complete details on this subject are presented later in the risk-management section of this chapter. Even without the details here, you can figure that the costs of malpractice, worker's compensation, and property/casualty coverage will be a substantial part of your annual business expenses.

13. POSTAGE

A stamp or two may seem inexpensive, but the costs add up fast! If you plan an introductory letter or brochure campaign or a quarterly newsletter mailing, carefully calculate the postage based on the weight of each item. While bulk-mail permits reduce per item costs on large mailings they also involve certain restrictions (check with the post office for bulk mail rules). Keep in mind that overnight shipping services and the post office offer business accounts for overnight delivery.

14. Wages, Payroll Taxes, Benefits

The real cost of each employee is the sum of the base wage plus payroll taxes plus benefits. Your accountant will know how to properly calculate the payroll taxes and can assist you in making these estimates. A small or new practice usually offers minimal if any employee benefits beyond those mandated by state or federal law.

15. Tithe

Since christians are familiar with the 10 percent tithe on income, it is not unusual for a Christian counseling group to include a tithe in the business budget. An alternative, especially in the early days when income is slim, is a tithe of time. It is my belief that we owe some of our God-given talent to be used for those who cannot otherwise afford counseling services. In private or group practice, the time tithe is a commitment to provide a set number of appointments at no charge for needy persons. A time tithe can also be given in training, teaching, and supervision. Although the time is not a true budget item, a side note of how many hours you give each year can be a great boost to your spiritual morale.

16. Unexpected

No matter how carefully you budget, some unexpected expenses will happen. Keep as much cash reserve as possible either in your business account or available from family reserves as a personal loan to your business. Never plan to spend every dollar committed to the business start-up.

Reserves for Survival

Self-employment specialists Sarah and Paul Edwards compare

starting a business with raising a child: "You have to support it until it can support itself."[3] This is the economic version of a paradoxical intervention. How can a new business support itself until clients come in and fees are collected? The answer is cash reserves. There are three basic approaches by which small businesses are kept afloat during the perilous period between start-up costs and cash flow from services.

TRANSITION INTO PRACTICE USING OTHER INCOME

Many counselors begin their careers as employees in mental health agencies, schools, or hospitals. For others, counseling serves as a second career into which they will move after leaving current jobs in other fields. If you are very low on cash, keep your present job and work with another counselor or group. In this way, you also preserve your company benefits (i.e., insurance, retirement plan, vacations) while you are building a counseling practice. It is pure folly to believe you can launch your own business with no savings, only limited credit, and no supplemental income.

An added advantage is that you eliminate many startup expenses during this early phase by working from another counselor's office. That probably means you will work several evenings, Saturdays, or other days off from your regular job. During that time, avoid making new financial commitments and save as much from your regular paycheck as possible. Combine this with strong efforts to promote your practice and you will see measurable results in income and referrals. That is the time to update your business plan and prepare to make the career move. If you have been valuable to your previous company, keep the doors open for part-time work or occasional work as a consultant. Every predictable income cushion is a blessing when you are newly self-employed.

REDUCE LIFESTYLE COSTS

A new business is an investment for the future. Think of it as "save now, enjoy later." Admittedly this is a tough concept for baby-boomers and post-boomers to grasp, yet materialism was not born in the eighties. No, this constant battle of discipline versus instant gratification is simply part of our humanity.

Even if self-discipline is the only asset that supports your dream of a counseling practice, it is the foundation on which business success blossoms and thrives.

With the cooperation of the entire family, make a plan to reduce your regular lifestyle costs. That means a reduction in nonessential expenses: eating fewer restaurant meals, opting for video rentals instead of amusement park tickets, limiting clothing purchases, eliminating impulse buying, and paying off all credit card debt. Divide the money you save between debt reduction and saving for the new business start-up costs. You can make it a challenge, rather than a chore, by getting the whole family excited about new alternatives for entertainment and shopping. If you are not sufficiently committed to your dream you will not be able to accept sacrifices in preparation. If this is the case, then you need to reconsider your priorities. Developing a new business begins with a financial, personal, and work commitment that many otherwise competent people cannot sustain.

Savings and Investments

If your family already operates in a low-debt, cash-efficient manner, then you are probably ready to begin prefunding your proposed practice. Make a structured savings plan that divides your average monthly surplus into two accounts: a family emergency fund and a business savings fund. An ideal financial planning formula is to keep available the equivalent of three months of necessary living expenses in an interest-bearing money-market account and place additional funds in potentially higher earning accounts that may not be as liquid (quick to access). Evaluate your investment plan the way holders of the Certified Financial Planner license do, according to these six portfolio considerations:

- **Time** for your investment to grow until you need the money.
- **Liquidity and marketability** that give a degree of access to your money.
- **Investment attitudes** that govern how you make investment decisions.

- **Risk tolerance.** Can you accept low, medium, or high risk to your principal investment?

- **Diversification.** These are strategies to avoid putting all your eggs in the same basket.

- **Tax consequences.** Minimize the tax bite from your savings.[4]

Investments are like a fertile garden of plants that need to be well-selected, carefully tended, and ready for harvest in the right season. Watch out for the high-flier, hot-tip, cannot-lose idea. If it sounds too good to be true, it probably is! "A faithful man will be richly blessed, but one eager to get rich will not go unpunished" (Prov. 28:20). The quick fix is not an investment—it is gambling.

RISK MANAGEMENT

From the time you awake each morning until you return to your bed each night, you live a life of risk. Many risks are unseen: the flu virus that you missed inhaling or the car radiator that nearly overheated just before you found a parking place. Other risks are heart-stopping realities: the errant baseball that shatters a window mere inches from your baby's playpen or the speeding car that recklessly cuts in front of you. Because risk is an inevitable factor in our world, we must choose to accept the full burden of possible losses or transfer some portion of the losses through insurance.

In business planning, the most costly risks include lawsuits for malpractice, injuries to workers or clients, damage to office property, theft, and loss of income due to an accident or illness. Some larger businesses choose to self-insure and accept the total financial burden of various risks, however, this is not practical for most counseling practices. The alternative is to transfer the risks to insurance companies that specialize in each area. Your premium payment buys peace of mind that your savings and hard work will not be wiped out by forces beyond your control. There are two types of loss claims to consider. If you fall on a loose floorboard in your office and break your leg, that's a first-party claim. When the same accident happens to a client, that's a third-party claim.

Risk management is easily explained in a restatement of the serenity prayer: Insure the risks you cannot manage, accept the risks you can afford, and have the wisdom to know the difference. As discussed in chapter 5, consult with a Chartered Life Underwriter (CLU) or other experienced risk-management specialist for the appropriate amount of coverage and ways to reduce risks in your office. You decide how much risk you can afford by the size of the deductible. If you can pay more out-of-pocket costs (deductible) before insurance reimbursement begins, your premium costs will be much less than if you have a low deductible. Here's a brief description of the types of insurance needed to deal with the business risks of counseling:

Professional Liability

Professional liability insurance covers your defense against claims of poor treatment, harm to the client, and alleged or real mistakes. From the first time you sit with a client during a graduate school practicum all through your career, professional liability insurance is necessary. A survey of several psychology practitioner liability insurers indicates that the leading causes of claims against counselors are: sexual misconduct, mistreatment, breach of confidentiality (that violates state statutes), inaccurate diagnosis, adverse consequences of dual relationships, fee disputes, involuntary confinement, slander, suicide or suicide attempt, misrepresentation of credentials, and failure to report child abuse.

Several counselor associations offer professional liability plans tailored to different workstyles (part-time, full-time, self-employed, employee, licensed, or intern). Limits of liability under the policies range from $250,000 up to $3 million. A licensed counselor must maintain high coverage (usually $1 million to $3 million) to be allowed to treat clients in a hospital or nursing home. But more is not necessarily better. Consider the type of practice you have and purchase the amount of coverage you need for the type of work you generally do.

When your policy arrives, READ IT. You need to be informed of the limits of coverage, who to contact for questions, and what out-of-pocket costs you might have to pay if sued. As added protection, read or attend programs on risk-management methods to learn how to protect yourself from claims. If you have a question or concern, call the insurance company's policyholder service department for further explanation.

PROPERTY AND CASUALTY

Whether you own or rent your office, losing that work space for any unscheduled period of time effectively puts you out of business. Just as you insure your home against fire, theft, vandalism, and other perils, so you need to insure the office in which you earn your paycheck. Most counseling offices are leased and covered by renter's insurance, but don't make the mistake of expecting your landlord to insure anything more than the building. As the tenant, coverage for the contents of your office (furnishings, equipment, art, client records, personal property) is your responsibility. Office tenants also bear the burden for injuries to clients inside the counseling offices. The tenant insurance package is similar in coverage to homeowner's coverage, except that it is designed to protect the renter, not the building owner. If you or your group owns the office building, a more comprehensive building-plus-contents policy is needed.

Be aware that any substantial improvements or additions you make to the rented office may not be covered by your tenant's policy. Even if the landlord approves, the changes may not be covered under the landlord's policy either. Your best protection for substantial office improvements is to purchase added coverage with a building-additions-and-alterations endorsement added to the basic tenant policy.

It is also important to ask your insurance agent about replacement coverage for valuable papers or files. This is part of or an addition to basic coverage; it pays for reconstructing files that are damaged or destroyed. Counselors in Florida's Dade County can tell horror stories of trying to get back to work after the wind and water damage from Hurricane Andrew soaked and damaged client files. Other files were literally blown away. And weather disasters aren't the only ways to lose files. A broken water pipe, a leaky roof, or smoke damage from a fire will make you thankful that you added file replacement coverage to offset some of the costs of restoring damaged records.[5]

Umbrella Coverage

This added coverage shelters you from a hailstorm of high losses. Also known as excess-liability policy, the umbrella policy supplements basic property coverage by meeting losses in ranges of $1 million and more (depending on your coverage choice). Insurers require that your property coverage meets minimum limits before umbrella coverage can be added. Carefully evaluate the worth of this coverage based on what it does not pay. The exclusions from coverage are professional liability, worker's compensation disputes, punitive damages, or any intentional act. However, some umbrella policies do protect you while you are acting in the role of a trustee or board member of a civic, charitable, or religious organization. As suggested earlier, in a church-linked counseling center, some type of umbrella coverage is essential to attract and protect your board or trustees. As you consider this type of coverage, shop cautiously to be certain that the umbrella you buy extends coverage without costly, wasteful duplication.

Computer and Equipment Coverage

Today's electronic office equipment is expensive to replace. The most valuable property in your counseling office is likely to be the computer, laser printer, fax, copy machine, and telephone system. Yet the standard contents or personal property coverage is not usually sufficient to protect your total equipment investment. So you might want to purchase a computer equipment policy or an endorsement (if available) to your basic tenant's policy. Keep a detailed list of electronic office equipment with serial numbers to back up any claims or aid identification and recovery if stolen.

Worker's Compensation

Each state establishes minimum standards of coverage for worker's compensation. As an employer you will want to know those standards and remain in compliance. The employer who fails to provide mandated coverage is subject to fines and legal penalties. Your state sets rules defining who is an employee, what types of work are exempt, and the level of medical or rehabilitation treatments that must be provided. For example, in my state (Florida) any employer with four or more employees must cover all employees under worker's compensation even if some work only part-time. A detailed procedure for filing worker's compensation claims is also spelled out in your state's rules. An employee can only make claims for injury or illness that is work related. The full cost of this coverage is paid by the employer and obtained in one of three ways: (1) By purchasing a policy issued by an insurer approved by your state employment division; (2) By joining a group of self-insured funds; or (3) By qualifying to self-insure by meeting the financial bonding and other rules of your state. With regard to the final method, don't decide to self-insure and then hope nothing adverse happens simply to avoid premiums. That approach may be illegal in your state and certainly is foolish from a risk-management perspective.

Health Insurance

Health-and-accident or health insurance refers to a range of insurance plans to protect the insured against economic consequences of illness, injury, and disability. Medical expense plans cover hospital services, surgical costs, physician care (inpatient or outpatient), and certain prescribed treatments. A new twist on health coverage for the group or business is through service providers like health maintenance organizations (HMOs) or preferred provider organizations (PPOs). Service providers are not insurers, but rather gatekeepers of medical care services that are purchased by subscribers. HMOs deliver a wide range of healthcare services that are prepaid by subscribers (individuals or companies) and provided by a network of private physicians or from salaried physician-employees working in the HMO facilities. The HMO goal is to encourage preventive care and thereby reduce critical care. A PPO is an organized group of private-practice healthcare providers and hospitals offering services to subscribers at reduced prices on a pay-as-you-go rather than a prepaid basis. Employees of companies that have a PPO contract are not required to use PPO providers. However, obtaining services from outside the provider network means more cash out of pocket. For example, a PPO might pay fifty dollars for a counseling session with PPO-approved licensed mental health providers but only twenty-five dollars for a session with a non-network counselor. There is always some financial incentive to use the PPO providers.

If you think this is complicated, we have not even looked at all the private insurance options, limits, and insurability factors that make health coverage so confusing to the average consumer. Before you commit to offer health insurance as an employee benefit, study the long-term costs. Is it feasible for your counseling center to pay health insurance for all eligible employees? If the number of your employees is too small to qualify for more favorable group rates, can you get health insurance for your employees as members of a larger group? For example, some counselor organizations and small business associations offer the advantages of large group rates for employers with fewer than ten employees. Even after paying the organization membership dues plus the insurance rates you may be dollars ahead of trying to buy direct health coverage for a small number of employees.

Health insurance, a costly benefit, is beyond the means of many new businesses that are short on cash. Be very careful about paying your own health insurance premiums out of company funds when you do not provide the same benefits to employees. Under some conditions this leads to major income tax problems. Your attorney and accountant can help you determine if your business structure allows for payment of health coverage and if employees must be included.

Disability Income

The risk of disability is often understated in seemingly *safe* jobs like counseling. Granted you are not dodging massive steel girders as construction workers do, but regardless of the cause, any injury that prevents you from working creates a simultaneous strain and drain on your personal resources. The strain comes from medical expenses and the extra burden of care your family endures. The drain is the loss of income for a lengthy period of time. A disability of even three to six months can destroy a counselor's practice and his or her family's financial security. After all, you cannot call a "rent-a-temp" counselor to take your place. With only a few months' absence your clients will seek other counselors and your referral base will dry up. Then when you return to work, you will have to rebuild your practice from scratch. This worst-case scenario is meant to demonstrate the importance of disability income coverage for counselors.

Disability income insurance pays a stated percentage of your former earnings for a specified period according to the definitions of the policy. The definition of the disability is critical. Coverage for *any occupation* means that you must be totally disabled for any possible job. Even if you are a Ph.D., you can be required to count widgets or perform any job for which you can be retrained. Your interests are better served with an *own-occupation* definition of disability. That means you are eligible for benefits if you are unable to perform the duties of your job (counseling) due to illness or injury. Own-occupation coverage is more selective and slightly more expensive; however, you get better rates if you can afford to accept a longer elimination period. The elimination period is the 60, 90, or 120 days you wait to receive benefits after the disability occurs.

Don't be lulled into the assumption that your disability losses will be handled by social security disability income (the OASDI program). The social security definition of disability is even more difficult to meet than that of the average any-occupation policy. The physical or mental disability under the social security definition must be so severe that it prevents any gainful work and lasts for twelve months or results in premature death. You would have to wait five months to qualify, and the first benefit for the sixth month would not be paid until the seventh month. Meanwhile you are forced to live off your savings, sell investments, liquidate retirement accounts, and mortgage your house to survive until social security disability payments begin or you qualify for other medical assistance. If you fail to qualify for this extreme eye-of-the-needle definition, you can easily lose your home and everything you own.

While counseling is not a physically high-risk occupation per se, any of us can suffer a short-term disability from totally unexpected circumstances such as injuries in an auto accident, an emergency surgery with lengthy recovery period, or contracting malaria on a missions trip. A few years ago, I slipped in my kitchen and tore a tendon in my ankle. During the six weeks I was on crutches, I could not walk up the stairs to my counseling office. Under normal conditions, the lack of an elevator in the two-story building was inconsequential; but when I had to walk on crutches, those stairs were as daunting as Pike's Peak. Needless to say, even that short-term disability had a negative impact on my income. Likewise, there are dozens of unforeseen risks to your personal health that could take a toll on the future of your counseling practice. You will be dollars ahead by deciding to transfer the impact of that risk through disability income insurance.

Auto and Life Insurance

Automobile insurance and life insurance are usually in place in some form before you begin a new business. With or without a business structure that provides this coverage, they are your personal responsibility. Providing this coverage as a company benefit within a typical counseling practice is not commonplace. Changes in tax laws have limited the opportunity to let your business pay these otherwise personal expenses. As discussed in comments on health insurance, consult with your attorney and accountant on what insurance coverage is appropriate and legally deductible as a business expense. After that question is answered, you will be better informed to contact insurance agents who specialize in each area for bids.

Budgeting Your Time

As a counselor, your primary business inventory is your time. Service providers who are paid a fee based on time spent with a client clearly understand the old adage, "time is money." Therefore, your time needs to be budgeted and monitored as it directly relates to your cash flow. As you learn to be more time efficient, you tend to be more fully present in the counseling session. You eliminate those drifting thoughts of the upcoming group session for which you are not prepared or the report that is already a week late.

TIME AUDITS

Attorneys and accountants are admirably effective in documenting client contact and other work that adds up to billable hours. They do this by weekly time audits. You can initiate your own time audit to discover how many income-producing hours occur in each week. This type of audit also reveals what you do during non-income-producing hours. Are these tasks part of your marketing strategy that will generate new clients? Or are you reading journals, attending unnecessary meetings, and hanging out in the break room during a two hour lull between clients?

Fancy computer programs and expensive forms are not necessary for a time audit. All you really need is a piece of paper with a line for each quarter hour of your work day. Set up your own simplified code to reduce writing, then make entries during the day as often as possible so that you remember exactly what happened. Here's a sample entry:

Time Log	What Really Happened
9:00 c/J. S./appt.	called J. S. to set appointment, heard new problem
9:15	continued to discuss problem with J. S.
9:30 coffee/Ed	drank coffee with Ed, talked about cars
9:45 mail/ c/per	opened mail, made personal calls
10:00 s/ B. D.	counseling session with B. D.

Can you see any wasted time during that brief account? Unless this counselor bills for phone consultations, the client wrangled a free half-hour during the 9 A.M. call-back to schedule an appointment. This was not a crisis call, just a routine call-back that could have been handled in five minutes. Was a fifteen-minute coffee break really necessary just a half-hour after arriving at work? Rather than lingering over the coffee pot trading stories with Ed, it would have been more time efficient to socialize at lunch. Personal calls need to be brief and limited in quantity. If you run overtime due to personal calls, you will not begin the 10 A.M. session with B. D. on time. Once your schedule falls behind it is likely that you will be running late for the rest of the day. This is not a productive use of your time and it is rude to keep your clients waiting. Remember that even if you are self-employed, the productive time you waste is your own!

At the end of the audited week, color code your progress. Mark poor time use with a yellow highlighter and good time use with a green highlighter. Spread the time sheets for all five days out on your desk. Do you see more yellow or green? If yellow dominates, be careful: You are engaging in wasteful time traps. Green is the signal to move forward in practicing time-management techniques that gradually become good habits. The green highlight also indicates the percentage of time spent in key functions directly related to client service, business management, and marketing. Apply the eight-twenty rule in this way: Aim to spend 80 percent of your time in *green* functions and 20 percent of your time in *yellow* secondary tasks such as paperwork, meetings, or other low-productivity items.

Another time trap is failing to be in tune with your body clock. Are you a morning person? Or do you work best in the afternoon and evening hours? As much as possible, do not fight your internal systems. Rather, make every effort to schedule your appointments and other substantial work to match your most productive times. For example, the best time for me to tackle serious writing, treatment planning, and other mental work is from 5 A.M. to noon. Those are my hours of peak productivity; evenings are my least productive hours. So when I am called to speak, teach a class, or see clients during evening hours, I know I will need a twenty-minute nap in the afternoon to recharge my energy levels enough to meet the extended day. If you are an afternoon or evening person, look for ways to plan your most complex work during your peak performance hours. You will get far more accomplished in the allotted time and with less effort.

Do you manage appointment setting or do you let appointments manage you? If there are regular gaps in your work day this may indicate a lack of planning in appointment setting. While you may have a preferred scheduling system, let me suggest one method that has been helpful for me: Look at your day as if noon (lunch hour) is the midpoint with hours radiating above and below. When asked by a client what appointment is available on Tuesday, begin by offering 11 A.M. or 1 P.M. For the next call, offer 10 A.M. and 1 P.M. If you prefer to have the first hour of the day free for report writing and other mental work (not a coffee break!), then attempt to schedule the remaining afternoon hours before filling the 9 A.M. slot. Take the same approach for evening hours. Fill the earliest hours first in descending order (6, 7, 8 P.M.). Before you protest that your clients will never accept this system, give it a try. This type of schedule management will not only improve your productivity, it will also reduce your stress.

Both the sole practitioner and the group practice need a monthly practice utilization review (see Appendix K). What are the total hours spent in direct client services? How many hours are devoted to groups? In reviewing each type of service rendered, which are increasing and which are decreasing? What is the reason for the changes? What are the five most common presenting problems that your counselors are treating?

You may want to extend this review to some random sampling of cases. Or make a separate sheet listing nonidentifying demographic information such as the age, sex, and martial status of the clients treated at your office during the period of the review. Were these clients motivated to come to your counseling center by referrals, friends, advertising, or church affiliation? Are your billings primarily cash or insurance? If you file a substantial amount of insurance claims, how successful is the rate of collection and how long is the wait? Add any elements you think will contribute to a precise statistical view of your counseling business.

A competent counselor is a lifelong learner through continuing education and other professional development programs. Besides attending conferences, schedule for yourself some regular time to read journals and books. Envision how much you can learn and improve your counseling skills by investing just one hour every two weeks for reading. You can recover that much time by reducing coffee chats or coming into work a half-hour early. Another approach that is popular with commuters is to order tapes to listen to during the daily drive or ride to work. Do not wait to *find* time; *plan* time for professional development. It is an investment in your counseling and management skills.

The Principle of Highest and Best Use

Real estate agents give careful attention to determining the "highest and best use" for a property. Since time is an important part of your business inventory, adjust your schedule for the highest and best use of it. Here are three principles that can help: delegate, eliminate, and restructure.

To delegate is not to avoid. On the contrary, it is a time-tested biblical concept of involvement. When Moses was headed for career burnout, fortunately he listened to his father-in-law, Jethro, and delegated judges for routine cases while he served as the "Supreme Court" for the most complex cases (Exodus 18). In the Great Commission, Jesus delegated the work of preaching the gospel to His followers until the end of the age. Now do you feel better about delegating? Administrators sometimes fail to delegate because they have such a need to control everything or want to appear to be the busiest person in the office, which can actually be a poor-little-me approach to gaining sympathy or admiration for an exaggerated devotion to duty. It is also possible to become inundated with busy work because of a failure to prioritize tasks. These are all work dysfunctions that may have some basis in your personality or may just be the result of inefficient habits. Do any of these work dysfunctions apply to you? To delegate is to trust and to teach. If your employees are not trustworthy and teachable, why did you hire them?

Eliminate the slush piles on your desk and your calendar. Slush includes those low-priority, procrastination-enabling, nice-to-do-but-not-critical tasks. Easier-to-recognize slush comes in the form of junk mail, unread journals, and other mountains of trivia. Here are a dozen basic methods for eliminating slush in your work space:

1. As soon as you open an envelope take action or trash the contents.

2. Program your telephone with frequently called numbers.

3. Limit book and journal purchases to those most directly related to your practice.

4. Use color-coded files for each major project.

5. Clean out your briefcase weekly.

6. Learn when to say no to additional committee or civic assignments.

7. Avoid keeping copies of articles just in case you need them. Instead, note the source, author, and date on a file card or computer file under the overall topic (i.e., depression, teens).

8. Use your waste basket twice as often as your desktop.

9. Whenever possible, write a brief response at the bottom of a letter or fax and return it.

10. Close your door to reduce interruptions during your daily planning and study time.

11. Purchase office supplies, order lunch, schedule package pickup, and do anything else you can arrange by telephone to avoid spending prime work time driving or shopping.

12. Get rid of your desk and use a two-drawer file cabinet that doubles as an end table, or purchase an end table with drawers (reducing space for piles of files, etc.).

As a counselor you often support a client's desire to change harmful habits into healthy behaviors. Now it's time to practice what you preach by eliminating slush from your work day.

After eliminating and delegating as much as possible, you are ready to restructure those duties that are your responsibility. Start by changing your response patterns; act instead of react. When you establish action-oriented work patterns you have less need to react to sudden interruptions or unscheduled items. For example, rather than opening the mail as soon as it is delivered, do it at the end of the day. If returning routine calls between sessions frequently puts you off schedule, set aside one hour each afternoon for call-backs. Use some creative daydreaming to imagine a highly productive, low-stress, warm-fuzzy kind of day at your office. Next make a written schedule of that ideal day. How closely does your typical day match your ideal day? Make the necessary changes slowly and manageably. Build on your successes, just as you probably tell your clients to do. Each week identify and implement just one small change; restructuring your workstyle for greater efficiency and tranquility is a gradual process of changing old work habits that are familiar but no longer functional.

If you feel hopelessly stuck in piled-high-desk syndrome, calendar cluttering, or slush disorder, get help. In some metropolitan areas you can arrange for a workstyle makeover by trained organizational and time-management consultants, or you can attend seminars, read books, and listen to tapes as a self-help approach to budgeting your time. A less expensive alternative is the buddy system. Ask a counselor in your office or a friend in another profession to join in your quest for better work methods. As you monitor each other's efforts, be a kindly critic and constant cheerleader. This accountability and friendly cooperation will benefit both of you.

NOTES

1. H. W. Sweeny and R. Rachlin, *Handbook of Budgeting* (New York: John Wiley and Sons, 1981), 2. Copyright © 1981. Reprinted by permission of John Wiley and Sons, Inc.

2. Ibid., 607–15.

3. Sarah Edwards and Paul Edwards, *Making It On Your Own: Surviving and Thriving on the Ups and Downs of Being Your Own Boss* (Los Angeles: Jeremy Tarcher, Inc., 1991), 49.

4. CFP ™ *Professional Education Program Study Guide III* (Investment Planning) (Denver: College for Financial Planning, May 1991).

5. For more information on restoring damaged records see *Psychotherapy Finances* vol. 19 (March 1993).

Chapter Eight

Identifying Sources of Income

The worker deserves his wage.

1 Timothy 5:18

COUNSELING IS A HELPING PROFESSION. Because we who practice it have a servant's heart for the welfare of our clients, we occasionally forget that all God's children have to earn lunch money. And that means us! Setting fees and asking for payment are often stated as the most difficult aspects of building and managing a counseling business.

Private-practice counselors depend on the fees generated from clients and other direct services. Counselors in a nonprofit counseling center usually receive a salary. Yet, in both circumstances, the counselor must respond to inquiries about fees. No matter how much you dislike discussing fees, answer in a positive way to convey the impression that your services justify the fee. If your tone and body language is apologetic and pleading for acceptance, you will encounter more resistance and bargaining. Clients immediately sense when you are uncertain about the true economic value of your counseling services.

The basis for the economic value of your work includes what you have invested in academic training and prior counseling experience. For example, a master's or doctoral level counselor with several years of supervised internship has made an investment in his or her career of $30,000 to $100,000 and seven to ten years' work. Every client benefits from the sacrifices this counselor made in career preparation. With an attitude of service, praise God for whatever skills and training you received. You have earned the right to enter practice believing that you are worthy of your pay. You are.

DIRECT SERVICES

In a counseling practice, the primary sources of income for direct services are fees, insurance reimbursement, consultation or supervision, and testing. Some or all of these income sources are restricted to licensed professionals according to each state's statutes. In addition, certain types of testing, consultation, and supervision require minimum levels of education or professional license.

COUNSELING FEES

The philosophy and economic determinants of fees are different in private practice than in church-linked nonprofit counseling centers. So we will deal with these separately.

For private practice, the first step is to determine the actual range of fees charged in your community by counselors of comparable credentials. A national survey of 1,905 professionals revealed an average individual session rate of $80, with a median of $85 in metropolitan areas and $75 in small towns or rural areas.[1] Even if those averages match the fees in your area that does not mean this is the amount you will actually collect in a new practice. Five factors must be considered in establishing private-practice counseling fees:

1. Counselor's level of skill (bachelors, master's, or doctoral training).
2. Counselor's status: licensed, internship for licensure, or nonlicensed.

3. Years of experience or specialization.

4. Preference for cash payments or insurance assignments.

5. Financial capacity of your target market.

The last item is the most influential factor. No matter how skilled you are, you will have a tough time collecting $80 an hour in a target market where $200 a week is the average take-home pay. In lower socioeconomic areas, you have the choice of charging lower overall fees or using a sliding fee scale based on client income. A fee study by *Psychotherapy Finances* reports that 54 percent of the therapists surveyed, particularly marriage and family therapists, use some type of sliding scale. It was further observed that therapists in the East and the West are more likely to use sliding scales than in the South and Midwest.[2] Although female therapists tend to charge slightly lower fees for individual counseling than their male colleagues, the $40 national median fee for group therapy seems to be unisex.[3]

The fee you charge needs to be an amount that can reasonably be collected at each session and not dependent on insurance reimbursement. If the fee is not excessively burdensome, clients will be more cooperative about paying at each session. This pay-as-you-go policy is also applicable for practices that agree to file insurance as long as the client remains current on copayments.

Another factor in determining fees is how much you need to earn to support yourself, your family, and your business. Using round numbers for simplicity, let us say that you are maintaining a very low overhead so that the cost of sustaining your practice for one year is $10,000. That includes office rent, marketing, general expenses, and answering service (no secretary). You have determined that you need at least $30,000 income to equal your previous salary. That means you must earn $40,000 to cover expenses and income. Since most new practices have fewer consistent clients, let us say you average twenty hours per week of paid sessions. Then twenty hours times forty-eight weeks equals 960 sessions. Using forty-eight weeks allows for time away from your office due to vacation, sickness, continuing-education conferences, and holidays. An annual fee income of $40,000 divided by 960 sessions equals a rate of $42 per session. That is the minimum counseling fee you can charge to meet income and overhead expenses ($40,000) based on an average of 960 sessions per year. Note, that this calculation shows gross income and does not adjust for income taxes. Therefore, depending on your tax rate and other tax factors, you may need to earn $50,000 in before-tax dollars to equal $40,000 after taxes. This example gives a rough estimate of necessary earning and fee determination. (See Appendix J for more detailed analyses of counseling fees. Your financial planner or accountant can also assist in this calculation.)

Simply stated, private-practice profit is what's left over after subtracting expenses and taxes from income. For annual projections, calculate the number of paid client hours as a percentage of the total hours available for appointments. Remember to adjust the number of appointment hours for holidays, vacations, and any regular days or half days that you are going to take off from work for continuing education. Unless you are the only counselor for a thousand miles around, do not expect your appointment book to be filled instantly or consistently in the early years of your practice. Here is a realistic guideline:

	Year 1	Year 2	Year 3	Year 4
Percentage of paying clients	30–40	50–60	60–70	70–80

Be conservative in your projections. Canceled appointments and no-shows erode your income expectations and make the 100 percent billable and paid hours a mere fantasy.

Nonprofit counseling centers that are church-linked or separately managed have a different approach to fees. Although making money is not the primary purpose, the cost of doing business must come from somewhere. A typical arrangement is a sliding-fee scale based on client income. Frequently, these fees do not cover the real costs of operating the counseling center so supplemental donations or underwriting is necessary.

As part of nonprofit budget planning, it is important to know the actual hourly cost of providing counseling services.

Here is a basic formula:

$$\frac{\text{projected annual operating expenses}}{\text{number of weeks x number of counseling hours per week}} = \begin{array}{c}\text{Actual cost of}\\ \text{counseling session}\end{array}$$

In this calculation, use a realistic number of work weeks. After you subtract two or three weeks for vacation and holidays, plus time for sick leave or continuing education, the real number of weeks worked in the year is closer to forty-eight or forty-nine. Total counseling hours per week is derived by either adding the counseling hours of each staff counselor or by calculating a numerical average of all counseling hours. This equation can be adapted for monthly calculations of actual costs. A monthly operating budget review is especially critical in the first year of operation to make certain costs do not exceed income from fees and fund-raising. Here is a hint: To make projections based on an average month, use 4.3 weeks as the multiplier instead of 4 weeks. Note that 4.3 weeks times twelve months equals 51.6 (rounded off as 52 weeks) in a calendar year.

After you determine the actual cost of a counseling session at your center, look at how that cost is met. The critical variable here is the amount collected from each client. If your actual cost per session is $45 and the average client pays $20, how will you cover the additional $25 needed to meet operating expenses? The more clients pay toward the actual cost of services, the less cost that must be offset by donations or underwriting. However, if the mission of your nonprofit counseling center is to provide low cost services, then you must factor in enough time, personnel, and expenses for a major fund-raising campaign.

Along with the impact of actual costs, nonprofit counseling centers have four additional factors to consider in determining fees:

1. Counselor's level of skill (bachelor's, master's, or doctoral training).

2. Counselor's status (licensed, internship for licensure, nonlicensed paraprofessional, or pastoral).

3. Financial capacity of the target market.

4. Funds available to supplement the actual cost of counseling.

For nonprofit counseling centers, the last item is often the most influential factor. The level and amount of services that can be provided to clients depends on a successful annual fund-raising campaign, church missions support, or other community grants.

Insurance Reimbursement

All too often, new practitioners approach insurance claims with visions of payments dancing in their heads. Those of us who have experience with insurance reimbursement know that it can be more like getting paid by Scrooge than Santa. Claim forms must be meticulously complete, diagnoses substantiated, and service codes accurate. Even if you use a billing service, you, the therapist, are responsible for providing sufficient information to process each claim.

You can save time and frustration by verifying the limits of coverage with the insurance carrier before the first session with a new client. Train yourself or your secretary to ask new clients if they have insurance that covers outpatient mental health services. Write down the name of the insurance company, the client's identification number, the employer group number, the employer's name, and the insurance company's phone number as listed on the employee's card or benefits booklet. Inform a new client that you will verify the availability of coverage for counseling prior to the first session. Yes, this takes extra office time, which is a burden on the sole practitioner, however; precertification of insurance coverage is a proven method among hospitals and large medical practices to avoid running up big bills that turn into unpaid accounts. Here are the questions to ask:

1. Does the client have current insurance coverage?
2. What is the annual deductible? What portion of the deductible has been met?
3. Will this policy pay for outpatient mental health services?
4. What categories of providers are eligible for payment? (Licensed only or other paraprofessionals under the supervision of a licensed provider)?

5. What claim forms or supporting documents are necessary to submit a claim?

6. What is the percentage of reimbursement and what is the client's copayment (typical amounts are eighty-twenty or fifty-fifty)?

7. What is the annual or lifetime maximum on outpatient mental health benefits?

8. How much of that annual or lifetime maximum has this client used to date?

Of course knowing all this still does not assure reimbursement. Insurance companies scrutinize mental health claims with the intensity of a father checking out his daughter's first date. You must realize that most insurance companies work on the medical model that identifies and treats disease, rather than a preventative, wellness model. In addition, the cost of treating severe and long-term mental health problems is very high. Thus, many insurance companies place low annual limits on reimbursement for counseling.

Eligible providers for all types of third-party reimbursement may include all or only certain classes of professionals. Unless your state insurance law intervenes, in-state companies and those headquartered outside your state are free to define which providers are acceptable. In some cases the list has not changed for many years; thus, newer license categories are excluded. While insurers express dismay over high treatment costs, many still require a psychiatrist or psychologist to do therapy work that is otherwise acceptable under state statute to be rendered by licensed master's level providers. Or a company will accept a licensed clinical social worker but refuse treatment by a licensed marriage and family therapist even if both are licensed under the same state statute. This question of *parity*, or equal treatment for comparable licensees, is a major problem with Medicaid, Medicare, and some insurance carriers.

A crucial component of the documentation for insurance claims is the diagnosis. You must be qualified to make an appropriate diagnosis from either the *Diagnostic and Statistical Manual of Mental Disorders* (DSM-III-R) or *International Statistical Classification of Diseases, Injuries, and Causes of Death* (ICD-9).[4] If the insurance company's medical review board challenges your claim, you will have to back it up with assessments, session notes, and a monitored treatment plan.

To protect your financial interests, make it clear that the client is responsible for paying the copayment, unpaid deductible, and any amounts that are not paid by the insurance company for any reason. There are two approaches to dealing with insurance payments. The first is to follow the lead of many physicians by obtaining payment from the client for services as they are rendered and providing documentation for the client to seek insurance reimbursement. This approach is the most financially advantageous for the counselor's cash flow; there is no need to wait for delayed payments, there are no paperwork battles, no processing costs, and no accumulated bad debts from clients who ignore you if their insurance company denies the claim. Be advised that setting this policy in your office will probably deter some clients who, like you, cannot afford to wait for insurance reimbursement.

The second approach is to have the client keep current on copayments while the counselor files the insurance forms for the remainder of the payment. In this instance, the counselor bears the greater financial risk. If the client has not met the annual deductible, you need to collect the full session fee until payments equal the deductible amount. Caution: Only the reimbursement percentage is applied to the deductible in most cases. With an 80 percent reimbursement schedule, the client must pay for $250 of counseling fees to offset a $200 deductible. Watch your math on this one! Once you have filed claims for those fees up to the deductible amount and have encountered no problems, then file immediately for the next session. Filing only one treatment on a form is not a customary practice, and though the company may cringe, this process will give you a fast answer as to the likelihood of future reimbursements. If there is a problem with the insurance claim, you want to know it before the client runs up a large bill at your expense!

Another way to enhance your income with third-party reimbursement is to become part of a preferred provider network or other managed care provider contract. These networks essentially "rent" you and your facility to deliver services to subscribers at a controlled price. Typically you are contracted at a fixed rate per session and asked to accept a minimum number of network or managed care referrals. If your appointment schedule has enough vacancies to resemble Swiss cheese, becoming a network provider may bring the needed cash-flow boost. Caution: Do not overcommit yourself at the beginning. As your practice begins to grow, you may have to turn away higher paying clients to fulfill your provider contract. For example, if the network pays $35 per session and your regular session rate is $50, you earn 30 percent less for each network client.

If you work with managed care providers such as employee assistance programs (EAPs) and preferred provider organizations (PPOs), you will be required to provide documentation of diagnosis, testing, and treatment planning similar to that required by private health insurance. The first step to entering a managed care system is to become an approved provider. Managed care companies may limit the number of certain types of providers in an area or accept only state licensed master's or doctoral level counselors. Once you are accepted as a provider, your work and documentation must meet all the conditions set forth by the company. For example, you may be required to use a specific intake form (instead of your own form) and provide a detailed treatment plan. After completing the intake and evaluation, you will have to follow established procedures to get approval from the managing company for a specific number of sessions, or you may need to report progress after a certain number of sessions. Counselors who want to work extensively with managed care providers need to gain skills in brief therapy in order to give clients the best possible treatment within the approved number of sessions.

CONSULTATION OR SUPERVISION

Responsible counselors seek assistance from knowledgeable practitioners in a periodic or ongoing relationship. In states with licensure laws, the activities of counselor interns must be monitored on a regular basis by a licensed clinical supervisor who meets qualifications specified in state statute. Professional credentialing organizations also require supervision to affirm that a counselor has achieved the required level of expertise to earn a certain designation. On another level, qualified counselors serve as consultants to both agencies and individual counselors (consultees). The consultant may be called in to participate in case-management conferences, assist in diagnoses, demonstrate new techniques, or give expert opinions on the counseling center's programing.

Whatever role a consultant or supervisor accepts, he or she is usually paid an hourly rate or a monthly retainer. If you are qualified and willing to serve as a consultant or supervisor, expect to be paid at least the same regular hourly fee charged for a private-practice hour. Consultants usually travel to the consultee's office, so be certain all your time away from your practice is paid. Even a forty-minute round-trip drive to the consultee's office means you miss one hourly session. And if you spent two hours last week reviewing journals and preparing information to present at the case consultation, how will that time be compensated? The two-hour consultation fee must be worth the five hours invested (two hours in consultation plus one hour driving plus two hours in preparation).

Supervision of counselor interns usually takes place at the counselor's office and thus eliminates travel time. However, the extra hours that are spent preparing material to teach or reviewing interns' client files adds to the real value of the supervision hour. Rarely are supervisors adequately compensated for the total hours spent in both formal supervision and informal supervision (i.e., frantic phone calls or interns dropping by your office to ask for advice).

Before you accept consultation or supervision responsibilities as an income-generating option, count the cost of liability for these roles. In Law for the Christian Counselor, George Ohlschlager and Peter Mosgofian emphasize that a supervisor is "fully liable for all actions of the supervisee" who is also an employee and "liability is coextensive up through the entire chain of command" if the supervisor is hired by an agency. As a contractual relationship, "liability for consultation is more limited and relative" than that of supervision.[6] Because these roles compound your risk, ask your professional liability insurance carrier about any limitations of coverage that apply to working as a consultant or supervisor.

Another good source of information about consultation in a variety of treatment settings is contained in a special issue of the *Journal of Counseling and Development*, titled "Consultation: A Paradigm for Helping."[6]

TESTING

Tests and assessments are useful tools in therapy, career guidance, and relationships. You may determine a need for testing during the counseling process to confirm diagnostic assumptions or monitor treatment effectiveness. Or clients may request testing to help them select a college, retrain for a new career, learn more about their personality characteristics, or as part of premarital counseling. For some counselors, testing is a major source of income. (Ways to generate additional income through testing will be detailed later in this chapter.)

Keep a current assortment of test catalogs from the major testing suppliers. These serve not only as a source of information, but they can give you new marketing ideas. Besides, testing and therapy equipment catalogs are as much fun for counselors as toy catalogs are for children. You will notice that some companies offer a sample kit or individual test for examination. This is a cost-efficient way to try out the instrument and determine if you want to purchase more.

Look for an explanation of restrictions on the sale of test materials printed near the table of contents or the order forms. The American Psychological Association sets standards for levels of professional training required to use certain tests.[7] The following is an example of these limitations as reported from a joint committee of professional organizations:

> **Level A** can be adequately administered, scored, and interpreted with aid of the manual and general orientation to the kind of organization in which one is working (i.e., vocational proficiency test)
>
> **Level B** requires some technical knowledge of test construction and use as well as supporting statistics (i.e., interest inventories, personality screening inventories).
>
> **Level C** requires substantial understanding of testing, supporting psychological topics, and supervised

experience (i.e., clinical tests of intelligence and personality). These are appropriate only for persons with at least a master's degree in psychology and one year of supervised experience or for graduate students under supervision of a qualified psychologist.[8]

These interpretations may be rephrased or coded differently; however, they will appear in the test catalog of any responsible publisher. You also need to study carefully the test manual for instructions in how to administer, score, and report test results. In making the decision of which test to choose for a specific client, the test manual's information on reliability, validity, and applications for use is much more suitable than brief catalog descriptions or journal reviews.

In order to determine accurately what to charge for testing, you will need to consider these four costs: 1. Test material, 2. Time to administer the test, 3. Time to score it, and 4. Time to prepare and present the written report. This is why testing specialists charge $100 for a test that sells for $15 in the catalog—the difference is the cost of the counselor's time. If you use a test that is not strictly timed or does not require interaction and monitoring, you can start one client working in the test room while you work with another client for an individual session in your office. This procedure will maximize your time. With instruments that require full interaction, single-subject administration, or strict time monitoring by a qualified therapist, the price of your time is equivalent to the regular session rate times the hours needed to administer, score, and interpret the test. On the other hand, tests administered to a group can be done at a more favorable per person rate. Another cost-saving method for the client is to use prepaid answer sheets that are mailed back to the test source for computerized scoring. (For an additional charge, some tests offer a computerized score summary and narrative.) If you are trying to offer a competitive price for testing, the use of computerized scores and narratives can be less expensive than the cost of your time to produce a comparable report.

Unless you build a reputation as a test and assessment specialist with regular clients (i.e., schools or industries), your income from testing is bound to be incidental to other counseling fees. For clinical psychologists and other licensed professionals who present findings as expert witnesses in court cases, testing can be very profitable, but this is a difficult field for newcomers to crack. Only those "big guns" with the powerful ammunition of academic, professional, and publishing credentials make substantial regular income from testing conducted for court cases.

MARKETING YOUR SERVICES ON A LARGER SCALE

Once your schedule is booked solid for the week, you are in great financial shape, right? Yes and no. Even if you sustain a high collection ratio with minimal cancellations, there are only so many hours in the day you can work. This poses a limitation on the counselor that other professionals do not have. Physicians and dentists use nurses and assistants to help them work with three or four patients during the same hour, but counselors can only work with one client or one group during one time period. Since you can only work so many hours per day, it might seem that raising fees is the only way to generate an increase in income. Yet by doing this, you risk pricing yourself out of your primary market. A more effective way to increase your income with little or no added work hours is to market your services on a larger scale. In the following pages we will discuss a variety of income producing ideas that will be useful to counselors in various types of practices.

WORKSHOPS

This concept is different from the educational workshops discussed in chapter 6. After you have established your professional reputation and gained clients through free public workshops, you are ready to adapt this format for a more lucrative market. Let's begin with the assumption that you are a polished speaker, an informative teacher, and you have expertise that others consider valuable. (If not, skip this section; you are not ready!) First, you will want to select a topic that can be condensed or expanded to fit various time constraints.

Second, define a primary and secondary target market for your workshop. For example if the focus is on adolescent identity issues, the primary market may be guidance counselors and parents of teens with a secondary market of youth pastors and high school teachers. You will greatly reduce your marketing costs if an existing group (such as your church or a parent-teacher association) agrees to host your presentation at its facility with its members as the core audience. For an incentive, you could offer a lower per person fee to the host group members than is charged to the public or at the door. Another alternative is for the group to pay you a flat speaker's rate to make a presentation to the membership. If you are speaking at a school, you can suggest to the principal that your program is suitable as in-service training for the faculty. These approaches adapt to the topic and target market of your choice.

If you have the proper credentials and experience, prepare a more sophisticated version of your workshop for professional and pastoral counselors. In this situation, you will want to focus on ways to identify and deal with a given issue from the counselor's perspective. Be prepared to justify your recommendations with academic and experiential data, and remember that counselors are a demanding audience who expect to be challenged, motivated, and inspired by your presentation. They also want opportunities for discussion and interaction. To be successful in this market, you must offer more than a rehash of old theories or pop psychology. The value of such workshops will be further enhanced if you qualify as a continuing-education provider either through your state professional regulation board or through a national counselors organization.

Therapeutic Products

Have you created a useful resource to facilitate therapy for a specific problem? Do other counselors marvel at your ability to synthesize information in a simplified format? Turn your innovations into therapeutic products that will benefit others and increase your income. The best potential products are those that develop as a response to a need. However, it is not a fast-track process. Generally the initial effort is small and requires several revisions before it is ready for appropriate field testing and evaluations. Yet, there is a voracious demand for all types of therapeutic products. And if your product addresses a special demographic group or presents a new approach, it can gain notice much faster. Some therapeutic products that are frequently developed include workbooks, test materials, and charts.

1. Workbooks. After several years of counseling prospective adoptive parents and women who make adoption plans, I developed a repertoire of effective adoption processes. It was a logical step to develop those yellow-pad-sessions into a workbook. Since its debut as part of several adoption counseling presentations, *A Special Plan* (a workbook for birthgivers) has sold to a limited market of adoption-triad counselors. Again in response to a need, I developed *A Special Blessing* (a workbook for adoptive parents) from still more client sessions. Thanks to desktop publishing on my office computer, favorable rates from a print shop, and binding done by my husband, the initial test marketing of these workbooks began with minimal investment or inventory. At this early stage the workbook price and profit margins are moderate, but possibilities are being discussed that will offer wider markets and perhaps lead beyond self-publishing.

These books were a pet project that resulted from an inherent belief in managed overhead. Producing these workbooks on a small scale allowed me to use and revise these resources in response to what I learned from actual counseling experiences. And the feedback and suggestions made by clients have proven invaluable. In brief, producing smaller quantities allows for economical revisions, so unless you have money to burn and an ego the size of Antarctica, stay away from the vanity presses and other high-quantity book publishing deals. Choose instead to build your market with patience and persistence. Otherwise, all you will build is an addition to your garage to store hundreds of unsold workbooks.

2. Test Materials. After emerging bleary-eyed from the final exam in Tests and Appraisals, did you wonder what latent rap poet devised all those Ts, Zs, Rho's and quartiles? Or do you speak psychometrics like a native? If you answered yes to the second question (no points for the first question), then your inquiring mind may be the source for a new test, an evaluation method, or an expanded use of an existing instrument. It is true that many instruments come from the academic community, which has the advantages of equipment, research grants, and graduate student assistants. So how can you compete? To begin with, do not compete on the same level. Tune your research-oriented brain to tackle a client-evaluation problem by developing a tool for counseling that is more user-friendly. A growing number of checklists and evaluation forms are being offered to assist the counselor in direct client work. These are practical treatment-planning tools that do not need complex designs or the type of analysis that would be expected for a psychological test geared toward diagnosis or personality disorders.

If you do create a testing instrument that requires the traditional reliability/validity studies, seek assistance from the psychology department at your local college or university. If you present your proposed project to the department chairperson or professor who teaches experimental psychology, there is a good chance he or she knows of a student or a study group looking for a way to fulfill a research project requirement. Such an arrangement would give you the benefits of academia and would provide the students with an experiential project. It is a win-win situation.

Once you have gathered data to back up the usefulness of your test or evaluation tool, you are ready to approach companies that distribute and market these products. By reviewing the test catalogs you can discover what types of instruments each company sells. Choose the three companies whose products most closely resemble your instrument and begin to make inquiries about submitting a product proposal. With a solid instrument and a confident presentation you will tip the scales in your favor.

3. Charts. Learning is enhanced by what we see as well as what we hear. So an orderly mind or an artistic hand that cleverly interprets information in visual form has potential for another type of therapeutic product—charts. Unlike graphs, pies or scattergrams, a chart is a less formal way to display data in a manner that is eye-catching and easily understood. Some charts portray desired behaviors. For example, a cartoon character can be used to depict both the correct and incorrect response to a situation. Charts showing expressions of feelings are available in cartoon faces and pictures of children or adults. Do you have a unique interpretation? Or can you convey biblical concepts about behaviors in an interesting pictorial form? Developing visual products for use in schools and counseling with children could be a lucrative market for you.

Charts have still more marketability as posters, T-shirts, and slides or transparencies. Posters can be a typical large size or as small as standard 8 1/2 x 11 paper. The reduced size of your poster can be silkscreened onto a T-shirt. A poster and matching T-shirts with a scriptural self-esteem message might serve as the theme for a youth convention or your next workshop. Test market these products on a smaller scale in your church and local Christian bookstores.

Slides and transparencies are an effective way to add visual impact and focus to your speech or teaching workshop. Once you have developed these tools, you could prepackage a generic script on stress management complete with visual aids and market it to other counselors. Specialized computer programs and photography equipment are available to use with an office computer and color printer; however, this setup is very expensive. Before you make a major equipment purchase, test market your idea. Most print shops have color copiers you can use to transfer your color designs to transparencies. Talk with camera shop personnel about the costs of making slides from your original designs or transparencies. Again, start small, test your product, and be prepared to make changes before the final version is ready to sell.

PRINT PRODUCTS

If your initial efforts with the issues-oriented brochures presented in chapter 6 work well, you might consider expanding your market with additional brochures, newsletters, and booklets. Not all counselors have a flair for writing, but if you do, you can combine your creative talents with your counseling experience to prepare marketable print materials.

1. Brochures. Incorporating what you know about brochure formats (see chapter 6), how can you appeal to a wider market? First, determine the scope of your topic. There are topics of general interest (i.e., codependency or stress) or those targeted to specific disorder (i.e., how to cope with your toddler's separation anxiety). Second, develop topics built around a common theme (i.e., healthy Christian families). Third, define the subgroups for whom brochures on each topic can be tailored. And fourth, if you use graphics coordinated with the central theme, keep them simple with clean lines that can be adapted for companion materials (i.e., letterhead, posters, and display cards).

Make sure the brochure text is free of any faddish phrases or colloquialisms that might limit its relevance for readers in other areas. Also brochure drawings or photos of people must match the ages, sex, lifestyle, and ethic characteristics of the comparable target market. A simple way to standardize graphics is with shadowed figures or silhouettes. Remember to leave space on the cover panel for personalization. A counselor who purchases your brochures will want his or her name, address, and telephone number displayed prominently on the cover. For an additional charge, you can offer to customize the cover information and add the return address and bulk mail permit number. Then all the purchaser has to do is address the brochures to clients and mail them. Or you could offer the brochure for a lesser price and let the purchaser have the customizing done by a local printer.

2. Newsletters. The four basics of creating a marketable brochure also apply to a newsletter. However, to simplify your beginning efforts, it is best to work with only one target market. The easiest place to start is with a market similar to your own client base. Generally, you need at least one year of experience producing a local newsletter for your own counseling practice before you have adequate feedback and experience to take on a larger project.

A newsletter provides a much quicker response to hot issues than a book or journal—a major advantage. And newsletters are more reader-friendly. Some of the most successful business-oriented newsletters synthesize major stories, give the results of trend studies, and rephrase complex government statistics into a collection of brief, easy-to-read items. Citations are given with each item so the reader can refer to the source for more details. Let your newsletter take advantage of a proven format and slant it for counseling issues and mental-healthcare news with a Christian perspective.

Your newsletter may also become the voice for a specific issue or support group. To find out if your idea is already being done elsewhere, peruse *Newsletters in Print*[9] at the reference department in your public or academic library.

Yet another way to market your newsletter is on a subscription basis. The added expense for you is in promotion, free sample mailings, or other means of generating subscribers. However, you do not even want to consider this project without extensive market research and a detailed business plan. A project of this magnitude and potential cost needs to be treated as a business in itself. Caution: The time spent producing and selling a subscription newsletter must be exceeded by sales. From a cash-flow perspective, if this is not feasible, choose the other newsletter marketing ideas or decline the publishing obligations and just schedule more client sessions.

3. Booklets. These mini-books allow space to cover a topic in greater detail than is possible in a brochure. You might want to offer a booklet with expanded information in a brochure of the same title. Use one panel of the brochure as an order form and sell the booklets for a nominal cost plus postage. Or you can sell the booklets or distribute them free of charge when you give a speech.

If you have a computer program that will allow you to develop a copy of the booklet that is camera-ready, you will save the cost of typesetting and arrangement. Or you can copy pages on a high-quality copier. For the cover, choose a slightly heavier stock (paper). You can add flair to your publication by selecting cover stock in a bold color, or, if you prefer, create an understated look by using a soft-color.

In addition to using booklets for more extensive treatment of issues-oriented material, this is also a good format for introductory topics. I developed an eight-page booklet that serves as the client information handbook for my Geriatric Skills Enhancement programs. It contains information about program entry qualifications, program rationale, billing, a brief description of core program modules, treatment planning, and a list of additional services. Since these elements cover the most commonly asked questions, the booklet serves as a handy reference guide for clients and their families. It covers the important inquiries but is still small enough to read quickly and easily.

You can adapt this booklet concept as an introduction to your counseling center, therapy groups, or other special programs. Perhaps you could write a booklet about a generic topic such as "Benefits of Group Therapy" or "The Importance of Premarital Counseling for Christian Couples" and sell it to other counselors or churches. (Remember to save room on the front and back covers for the user to print or stamp his or her name to customize the brochure.)

Packaged Products

Too often counselors think in terms of one service at a time. Why not develop a broader vision of your practice. Brainstorm for ways that your services could interrelate. To stimulate your thinking processes, here are four approaches to packaging therapeutic services and products in ways that are cost efficient for clients while increasing your income.

1. A battery of tests and a narrative report to match employees with specific jobs.
2. A battery of tests to be used in guidance counseling for high school juniors or seniors to measure occupational interest, study habits, and suitability for college.
3. Stress-management workshop materials with pre- and post-tests of stressful behaviors and individualized reports given to healthcare workers, business managers, or other employees in high-pressure occupations.
4. Parent workshops using your own material or under contract and training by existing resources such as STEP Parent Workshops[10] or Parenting Within Reason.[11]

There are many more ways to combine your expertise with therapeutic products. Since you spend only three or four hours with one group rather than thirty or forty hours doing the same work on an individual basis, you can charge a lower rate. But be aware of how many group members or packaged products are needed to equal your customary one-hour session fee. If you need four participants at $15 to equal your usual $60 session rate, then set five or six as a minimum to pay both your hourly rate and a little extra for transportation costs. Simple math shows that the larger the group the greater the financial return on your time—another win-win situation for you and your clients.

If you are already thinking of other ways to combine services, reach larger markets, and offer affordable testing or group programs, then you have caught the spirit of this chapter. Making your therapeutic resources and group programs available to other counselors and clients is a way of sharing your creative gifts. Whether you develop written resources or toys for the therapeutic playroom, the possibilities are limitless.

NOTES

1. *Psychotherapy Finances: Survey Report*, vol. 17, no. 12 (Jupiter, Fla.: Ridgewood Financial Institute, 1992), 1. For more information call 800-869-8450.

2. Ibid., 3.

3. Ibid., 1.

4. *DSM-III-R* is published by the American Psychiatric Association, Washington, D.C. *ICD-9* is published by the American Medical Association, Chicago, Illinois. Both publications are subject to periodic revision. Be certain you have the current copy.

5. George Ohlschlager and Peter Mosgofian, *Law for the Christian Counselor* (Dallas: Word, Inc., 1992), 280.

6. *Journal of Counseling and Development*, vol. 71, no. 6 (July/August 1993).

7. *Ethical Standards for the Distribution of Psychological Tests*, American Psychological Association, 1950.

8. Lorraine Eyde, Kevin Moreland, Gary Robertson, Ernest Primoff, and Robert Most, *Test User Qualifications: A Data-Based Approach to Promoting Good Test Use*, a report of the Joint Committee on Testing Practices, sponsored by the American Psychological Association, the American Association for Counseling and Development, the American Educational Research Association, American Speech-Language-Hearing Association, and the National Council on Measurement in Education (Washington, D.C.: December 1988), 19.

9. Brigette T. Darnay, ed., *Newsletters in Print,* 4th ed. (Detroit: Gale Research, Inc., 1988).

10. Don Dinkmeyer and Gary McKay, *STEP (Systematic Training for Effective Parenting)* books and teaching resources offered through American Guidance Service, 4201 Woodland Road, Circle Pines, Minnesota 55014-1796. Write for information about Leader Training Workshops.

11. Buddy Scott, *Relief for Hurting Parents* (Nashville: Oliver Nelson Publishers, 1989). For information about support groups and leadership training call 409-297-5700.

Chapter Nine

Business Tax Issues

Give to Caesar what is Caesar's, and to God what is God's.
                                                    Matthew 22:21

O<small>NE OF THE FEW ISSUES IN LIFE ON</small> which you get widespread agreement from both Christians and non-Christians is a mutual disdain for ever-increasing taxes. Like it or not, paying taxes is a citizen's duty. And the Bible adds this obligation for Christians:

> This is also why you pay taxes, for the authorities are God's servants, who give their full time to governing. Give everyone what you owe him: If you owe taxes, pay taxes; if revenue, then revenue; if respect, then respect; if honor, then honor. (Rom. 13:6–7)

Regarding our legal obligation to pay taxes, the late Judge Learned Hand gave some practical advice:

> Anyone may so arrange his affairs that his taxes shall be as low as possible; he is not bound to choose that pattern which will best pay the treasury; there is not even a patriotic duty to increase one's taxes.[1]

Judge Hand's opinion might be viewed as the forerunner of modern tax planning. This is something you can't ignore because failure to manage assets for maximum benefit to yourself can tax the life out of your counseling business.

Tax Planning

What You Need To Know

When you ask the average business person how he or she handles tax planning the typical response is, "my accountant does it." Wrong! Accounting deals primarily with the history of canceled checks; tax planning is future-oriented. So unless your CPA is very skilled in tax planning and works with you regularly on this task, you are merely reacting to a tax bill rather than acting to lower your tax burden.

By the time you bring ledgers, bank statements, and other documents to your accountant for tax preparation, those documents are historical records of the past year's financial transactions. Once the year is over, so is your opportunity to reduce your business taxes. So unless you seek the services of an experienced tax planner at the beginning of a fiscal year, all you are likely to get is accounting, tax forms, and a bigger tax bill than necessary. Tax planning begins in January and continues throughout the year. The key to successful tax planning is monitoring and proactive decision-making in the present that will lead to a desired future result.

Regardless of how expert your accountant or tax planner is, you need to be familiar with the tax rules that apply to your business. Concentrate only on the rules for your business structure and your individual tax status. The good news is you do not have to struggle through the tax code books to learn what is useful in your business. While those weighty texts may cure your insomnia, there are easier, more informative resources. An excellent primer is the free IRS Publication 334, *Tax Guide for Small Business*.[2] A condensed desk reference resource that can be understood by a layperson is the annually updated *U.S. Master Tax Guide*.[3]

You will see a lot of references to free IRS consumer publications in this chapter. I have chosen to recommend these reader-friendly publications instead of the complex tax code books. A full list of IRS publications and ordering information is detailed in Appendix A.

Do not be discouraged if you cannot read a tax form past the line with your name and address, the IRS will teach you. Study samples of completed returns from a sole proprietorship, partnership, S-corporation, and C-corporation printed in the *Tax Guide for Small Business*. Detailed explanations accompany each sample business tax form. Another way to learn about tax issues pertaining to your business is from another free IRS Publication 910, *Guide to Free Tax Services*. You can attend free or low-cost seminars on business tax issues sponsored by local or regional affiliates of the Small Business Administration (SBA). Also some local chambers of commerce conduct periodic seminars on tax planning and recordkeeping for small businesses. Other classes on business taxes for nonaccountants are offered in adult education classes and evening college programs. Once you realize how much help is available, any further protests are going to sound akin to therapeutic resistance. So consider yourself confronted with the facts. Regardless of how expert your accountant is, you need to be able to read your business tax forms and know what applies to your situation.

Another important concept to grasp is that all dollars are not created equal. There are before-tax dollars and after-tax dollars. Using a very simple example, each before-tax dollar is worth only seventy-two cents after taxes when applying a 28 percent income tax rate with no deductions. So a dollar that is taxed does not buy a full dollar's worth of goods or services. Now you see where your money goes! A critical aspect of good tax planning for you, the business owner, is to calculate how much you must earn in before-tax dollars to provide the necessary after-tax-dollars to meet your needs and to support your family. A standard piece of advise, depending on your business structure, is to pay as many bills as allowable with before-tax dollars. You may need some help from your accountant to separate business from personal expenses and calculate your gross income requirements, however, it is in your best interest to learn how to apply these concepts in practical ways in order to get the most out of tax planning in daily business decisions.

What you spend for your business is not always as vital as when you spend it. Timing business expenditures is an important part of tax planning. If your income for the first year of operations is low but shows measurable increases (not wishful thinking), delay major purchases until the second year, when income reaches a higher tax bracket.

Partnerships and corporations are required to apply for an employer identification number (EIN) by filing Form SS-4. If a sole proprietorship has any employees, it also needs an EIN. The EIN must appear on all income tax returns, tax payments, or other communication with the IRS. Banks, investment accounts, and other business transactions also require your EIN. A sole proprietor who does not have employees only needs to use his or her social security number for tax reporting as a self-employed individual.

RECORDS MANAGEMENT

When you stop to consider the recordkeeping responsibilities in all business structures, no doubt you will agree that paperwork is the eighth deadly sin. However, this vice (paperwork) becomes a virtue (records management) when it is set up in an organized system. Not only are accurate records vital for efficient business operations, but they are required by the IRS to support all items of income and expenses reported on your tax return.

Business records need to be updated no less than monthly. This includes reconciling the business's bank statement and posting payments on each client's ledger card. The question of how long to keep business records is subject to different answers depending on who you ask, but according to the IRS, you must keep all supporting records related to a tax return until the statute of limitations runs out, which is "the later of 3 years after the date your return is due and filed or 2 years after the date the tax was paid."[4] However, it sometimes takes more than three years for the IRS to send one of those "Dear Taxpayer" letters questioning something on an earlier return. Be safe rather than sorry—keep tax returns, invoices for property on the depreciation schedule, payroll records, canceled checks, bank statements, records of investment purchase and sale, client ledger cards, and accounting ledgers (or ledgers on computer disc) as long as you remain in business, then up to three years after the business closes. The length of time you are required to retain client counseling records is governed by your state statutes. When the papers begin to overtake your file cabinet, pack away the oldest records in sturdy plastic storage boxes with watertight seals. Store old records in your attic, garage, or another accessible place. If you are challenged by the IRS or involved in litigation, you will be much better off with too many records than too few.

An excellent source of free advice on recordkeeping systems, check reconciliation formats, and simplified bookkeeping forms is available in IRS Publication 583, *Taxpayers Starting a Business*. This easy-to-read booklet also discusses methods for depositing taxes and using a Federal Tax Deposit Coupon Book.

Actual bookkeeping work and costs can be greatly reduced by the consistent use of a check coding system. Put the appropriate account code in the check register and on the lower left corner of each check that you prepare for your business account. Here is a simple version of the more complex account codes used by larger companies.

1. Advertising
2. Bank charges
3. Car expense
4. Counseling fees
5. Dues (memberships)
6. Insurance
7. Legal and professional services
8. Meals
9. Office expense
10. Postage or special mailing
11. Printing
12. Refunds

13. Rent or lease of property, vehicles, and equipment

14. Repairs and maintenance

15. Seminars and meetings

16. Supplies

17. Taxes and licenses

18. Telephone

19. Travel and lodging

20. Utilities

21. Wages

The categories are arranged alphabetically for easy retrieval. Alter or add to this list to suit your business and keep a copy of the codes in the front of your check register for quick reference. It is also helpful to add details on your checks for tax payments by using tax letter codes, such as FUTA (Federal Unemployment Tax Act), FICA (Federal Insurance and Contributions Act), WC (worker's compensation).

Equally important, you can mark deposit slips to indicate the difference between a regular deposit (DEP) and a nontaxable deposit (NTD). A nontaxable deposit can be a loan to your business or a redeposited check. Remember, nontaxable deposits are not income. Failure to mark those NTDs might result in reporting them as income, which is a costly mistake!

Quarterly reviews are the minimum necessary for good tax planning. This timetable also conveniently conforms to IRS quarterly payment schedules. If you have consistently used codes, you can quickly scan the deposit slip copies or your check register for the (DEP) code to calculate the actual amount of income earned.

To track expenses, make a sheet with the number codes and abbreviated titles. You can arrange these in columns on a legal pad or get fancy and use a multicolumn accounting pad. Under the heading (1) *Advertising* list the amount of each check with that code paid out during the quarter . Continue the process until all checks for the quarter are noted in the appropriate categories. At this point, you are simply looking for category totals, you are not scrutinizing the reason for the expenses. You will increase your accuracy by using an adding machine with a tape to check each category. When you have completed this process, retain each quarterly worksheet with the supporting receipts, invoices, and canceled checks in a file marked for that quarterly period and year, i.e., January-March 1993. To avoid losing items, place the smaller receipts in a marked envelope before putting them into the file folder.

A large corporation may require a more sophisticated system or one entered on computer, but for the average new counseling business, simple is better. If you are new to business accounting, avoid the temptation to rush out and buy a financial computer program. Remember, the computer will not help you do something that you don't really understand. With computers, it is always G.I.G.O. (garbage in, garbage out). That is a concept we recognize as counselors. After all, from a spiritual perspective it is the same way with people.

Tax Year

Although there is no way to avoid taxes, there are some choices about how your business defines its tax year. The IRS Publication 538, *Accounting Periods and Methods,* gives a detailed explanation of this subject. The basic periods are *calendar year* and *fiscal year*. The calendar year is exactly what it sounds like, January 1 through December 31. For most small businesses, a calendar year is the logical choice.

According to the IRS, you must use the calendar tax year under three conditions:

1. If your records are inadequate.
2. When you have not designated an accounting period.
3. Anytime your operational tax year does not meet qualifications for a fiscal year.[5]

A fiscal tax year contains twelve months that run consecutively. The fiscal year may not comprise the same twelve consecutive months as the calendar tax year, which ends on December 31. Due to the variations of time, a fiscal year may contain fifty-two or fifty-three weeks. You must formally declare your intent to use a fiscal year. Two forms that will be helpful in this regard are IRS Form 1128 *Application to Adopt, Change, or Retain a Tax Year* and IRS Form 8716, *Election to Have a Tax Year Other Than a Required Tax Year*. Both of these forms have detailed instructions, however, you need to consult your accountant before making this decision.

By rule, the fifty-two or fifty-three week fiscal tax year must end no earlier than the twenty-fourth day of the month and no later than the third day of the following month. Before you can change to a fiscal tax year that ends in a different month than your prior tax year, you must get written approval from the IRS.[6]

There is also a provision for a *short tax year:* a period of less than twelve months that occurs when the business has not existed for the full tax year or for that time before filing a change of accounting period. Knowing how to handle reporting for a short tax year can be complicated for a novice, so save yourself a headache—stick to counseling and take this problem to your accountant.

The Myth of the Independent Contractor

What You Need to Know

A lot of counselors think of themselves as independent contractors. Still other counselor-administrators say they have only independent contractors working in their offices. If I had a nickel for each of these situations in which workers failed to meet the IRS tests for independent contractor, I could retire from counseling and take a world cruise. Because this is such a widely misunderstood situation, I will discuss the independent contractor issue separately for emphasis. What you read here (and confirm later with your accountant or tax specialist) may save you a 100 percent tax penalty or more!

What is your definition of an independent contractor? Some people will say there are three tests or four tests or six tests to pass in order to be an independent contractor. Others say that if an employer agrees to your contract and payment terms, that is enough to qualify you as an independent contractor. All of these answers are WRONG. There are twenty factors that must be met, and guess who grades the paper: the IRS! In other words, you either score twenty out of twenty or your independent contractor becomes an employee. That transformation is instantaneous and retroactive, and the employer must assume full responsibility for employment taxes, withholding, and other reporting requirements. This usually stretches the financial capabilities of a new counseling business.

It is easy to understand the counselor-administrator's preference for classifying an associate counselor as an independent contractor to avoid paying state unemployment tax, FUTA, matching FICA, and other required reporting. The difference between paying employee taxes or paying straight fees to an independent contractor ranges from 10 to 15 percent more expense to your business.

Actually the main issue is control. If you have any control over the person's work day, times, or choice of therapeutic methods, then the worker is an employee. By contrast, your attorney is an independent contractor providing service to the public for a fee. You hire the attorney to handle a specific job, however, you do not direct him or her in the performance of that work. Now before you try to rationalize how your counseling center's situation really does not involve control, don't forget the other hurdles, like the Twenty Factors Test.

THE TWENTY FACTORS TEST

In IRS Publication 937, *Employment Taxes and Information Returns,* a brief description is given for the twenty factors that determine if a worker is an employee or an independent contractor. These factors are summarized as follows:

1. Employer gives instructions or retains the right to control the work of an employee.

2. An employee is required to be trained in a particular manner.

3. An employee's services are integral to the continuation of the business.

4. An employee must render services personally, which shows that an employer is interested in both method and results.

5. An employer hires, supervises, and pays assistants for an employee. An independent contractor handles this matter under a contract.

6. An employee has a continuing work relationship with an employer.

7. An employee must work days and times set by an employer. Independent contractors set their own schedules.

8. An employee may be required to work full-time. An independent contractor decides when or if to work.

9. An employee's work must be done on the employer's premises or at a designated location.

10. An employee's services are performed in a certain order or sequence indicating employer control.

11. An employee submits regular reports to the employer.

12. An employee is paid an established rate for work by the hour, week, or month. An independent contractor is paid by the job or on a commission.

13. Business and travel expenses are paid for employees, not for independent contractors.

14. An independent contractor furnishes significant tools and materials for his or her work. An employee uses equipment provided by the employer.

15. The independent contractor's significant investment in his or her business must be shown.

16. An independent contractor has potential to make a profit or incur loss on the job.

17. An independent contractor provides services to more than one person or company at the same time.

18. The services of an independent contractor are available to the public and are not restricted.

19. An employee can be fired. An independent contractor

cannot be discharged from work as long as the result meets contract specifications.

20. An employee can quit a job. An independent contractor is bound by contract to complete the job or be subject to penalties defined in the contract or legal action.[7]

To apply for IRS approval of independent contractor status, you or your employee must file Form SS-8, *Determination of Employee Work Status for Purposes of Federal Employment Taxes and Income Tax Withholding.* Even if you as the employer make an advance filing to determine status, the IRS will contact the employee named on the SS-8 form for additional information. In this situation the IRS acts like a parent, separately taking you and your sibling aside to hear the story of how the baseball hit the window. Only in this case, you will be out of the game if there is just one strike or one wrong answer to any of the twenty questions on the SS-8 form.

And it gets worse! If your employee is denied independent contractor status, you will have to calculate the withholding and pay the taxes that are due. That is the cost of making an honest mistake. However, if the IRS decides that you had "no reasonable basis" for treating the worker as an independent contractor, you can be liable for a penalty equal to 100 percent of the taxes that were due but not paid—plus interest. That liability is also directed at the person designated to make the tax payments for the business, even if that person is a corporate officer, partner, sole proprietor, or an employee of the business.[8]

A LOSING BATTLE

Many counseling offices and nonprofit counseling centers follow the "don't ask, don't tell" rule. They "don't ask" for an IRS determination for fear of finding that their independent contractor really is an employee. Furthermore, they make the mistake of suggesting that their counselors "don't tell" about their work status. Unfortunately, if it is your business you risk becoming the scapegoat when a new counselor who failed to make his or her own quarterly withholding payments gets hit with the full taxes due and decides (irrationally) to blame you.

That (and other disgruntled worker situations) is how the IRS discovers many employees who are ineffectively disguised as independent contractors. Workers can take the initiative to file SS-8 forms and find out if they were properly classified as independent contractors by the employer.

When the other shoe drops and your counseling center gets a very terse letter from the IRS, be prepared to drain your checkbook of the taxes that were due—plus stiff penalties. The business owner or corporation is responsible for paying all applicable employee taxes whether or not the amounts that would be due from the employee have been collected. As the owner, you must pay the full amount due the IRS, even if you did not withhold the proper amount or did not make any withholding due to the incorrect assumption that the worker was an independent contractor.

Even if you take the assertive approach and file the form on behalf of your workers, you are playing against the Philistines without a slingshot. Several accountants warned us that SS-8 forms were not really meant to issue positive determinations. These forms are more commonly used to trap employers who have "no reasonable basis" for paying workers as independent contractors. We believed that the working relationship between our geriatric group therapy program and the Licensed Clinical Social Workers (LSCWs) under contract did meet all the tests. In fact, our contract with the LSCWs was designed to conform in all ways to the twenty factors outlined by the IRS.

We sought to be so precise in defining the "reasonable basis" for this status that we stated all twenty factors in the contract and explained how each applied to our program. The LCSWs contracted in our program also worked for one or more other companies and had prior experience working as independent contractors.

Feeling confident that we met both the letter and spirit of the law, we bravely filed an SS-8 form. We were denied on minor points. I will spare you the lengthy letters and months of telephone tag we spent battling the denial. In answer to our final appeal we received a long letter that quoted situations in revenue rulings that were not explained or easily available to the public. (Two nearby law libraries did not have all the rulings noted in that IRS letter!) The letter also compared our situation with IRS Technical Advice Memorandum 8749001, a case of home healthcare services that involved considerable reporting and control.[9] Our workers had no such requirements for reporting except those conforming to rules of the Florida Department of Health and Rehabilitative Services (charting at the nursing home), Florida Statute 490 and 491 (client record requirements), and Medicare or supplemental insurance (an encounter form indicating date, treatment code, diagnosis, service provider, and charges). When work was completed, the therapist submitted a bill for services at the contracted daily rate. The reporting to which the IRS objected was that required by federal (Medicare) and state (Florida) laws. The more questions we answered and defended, the more resistance we encountered. Finally, we gave up rather than hire an attorney and fight what was clearly a losing and increasingly expensive battle.

If this story sounds discouraging and the twenty factors seem impossible to meet, you are getting the message. The independent contractor status does not appear to be valid for many of the situations in which it is claimed by counselors, businesses, and ministries. Admittedly, some advisers and management books treat the independent contractor issue casually. We did not. And although we disagree with the IRS's denial for our contract workers, we do not regret getting the matter settled. Other counselors with less defensible positions than ours have told us that they will continue to overlook the problem unless forced to change. Unfortunately, that may well be a bankrupting change. And it is not honest. It is like saying that sin is not sin unless the pastor catches you doing it. God is forgiving and so is your pastor—but the IRS is not so forgiving.

Consultation or supervision seems easier to defend for independent contractor status as long as no controls are exercised by the hiring organization. Before you decide to treat any worker as an independent contractor, review the twenty factors and discuss the situation with your accountant. If anyone tries to tell you it is not really so complicated, they are gullible enough to buy an air-conditioning franchise in Iceland.

Sole Proprietorships

For many counselors initiating their first business, a sole proprietorship is the least expensive and simplest type of business operation to understand and administer. As a sole proprietor, you use your personal social security number for business tax reporting on Schedule C, *Profit and Loss from a Business*. Schedule C is attached to your regular Form 1040 income tax return. If you use the account codes and quarterly review system described earlier in this chapter (see Records Management) it will be much easier to complete Schedule C.

A sole proprietor is self-employed and must pay taxes as calculated on Schedule SE, *Self-employment Tax*. By answering the questions printed on the SE form, you will find out if you can use the short form SE or are required to submit the long form SE. In either case, the SE form is attached to your personal 1040. There are some exemptions from self-employment tax, including those related to ministerial income. Ask your accountant to carefully review the implications of this tax and whether or not you qualify in your counseling business.

To gain the most tax value from property used in your business, you must also file Form 4562, *Depreciation and Amortization*. This pertains to tangible property such as office equipment, vehicles, cellular telephones, computers, and some other types of property. It is extremely important to file this form correctly the first time to establish the depreciation or amortization. You must have receipts and accurate records to substantiate these items. Although there are explanations on the IRS form, this is a business tax issue that easily confuses new business owners and is best handled by an accountant.

The essential benefit of operating as a sole proprietor is the ease of starting, operating, and closing the business. No filing or fees are necessary to begin and the sole proprietor avoids the corporate problem of double taxation (personal income tax plus business income tax). Income and deductions pass through to the individual. By filing Schedule C, a sole proprietor can subtract all legitimate business expenses from business income and establish a net profit or loss. Only the net profit is taxed as income; net losses are reported but not taxed.

PARTNERSHIPS

As a business structure, a partnership is a separate entity from the individuals who own it. Yet for tax purposes, the partnership acts like a funnel that directs the income and losses of the business to each partner. Each partner receives a distributive share, or share of profits and losses, that matches his or her percentage of ownership in the partnership. Because of this pass-through effect, partnership income is not subject to double taxation. From a tax law perspective, a partnership must have no more than two of the four corporate characteristics: (1) continuity of life, (2) centralization of management, (3) limited liability, and (3) free transferability of interest. Caution: If a husband and wife jointly manage their counseling business and share equally in profits or losses, they may be viewed as a partnership even if no formal agreement exists.[10]

Partnerships file Form 1065, *U.S. Partnership Return of Income,* which is far more detailed than that required of sole proprietors. The personal tax return must also include a Schedule K-1, *Partner's Share of Income, Credits, Deductions, Etc.* Special directions on the far right side of each K-1 item indicate where this number must also be placed on corresponding forms, including the individual Form 1040, Self-Employment Schedule SE, or other forms named. Additional free information on reporting for this business structure is in IRS Publication 541, *Tax Information for Partnerships.*

An advantage of the partnership is that it provides a more formal business structure without the additional tax burden of a corporation. The partners choose the accounting methods, depreciation methods, and calendar versus fiscal tax year. If the partners are in similar tax brackets and financial life stages, they can make these choices to best complement their personal tax situations. Furthermore, tax laws provide for an orderly transition of control that facilitates the intent of the partnership agreement and by-sell agreement in the event of a partner's withdrawal, retirement, or death.

CORPORATIONS

Counselors who choose to incorporate generally use a Professional Association (PA) or Professional Corporation (PC) that conforms to the rules for corporate tax reporting. All corporations must obtain an employer identification number (EIN) by filing Form SS-4. The IRS treats all new corporations as C corporations unless a Form 2553 is filed to elect the S corporation status or to fulfill the requirements for nonprofit status.

Corporate tax accounting is far more complex than that for a sole proprietorship. Detailed documentation is critical for corporate reports both to the IRS and to corporate shareholders, which is why records management was emphasized first in this chapter. In ultra-simple terms, a C corporation is a separate taxable entity subject to its own tax rates whereas an S corporation allows for pass-through of income or losses to the shareholders. The S corporation is a hybrid that includes the organizational advantages of incorporation but without double taxation due to the pass-through of income and losses to each shareholder. The annual tax return for an S corporation is Form 1120-S. For detailed information, order IRS Publication 589 for S corporations. Now stay with me as I explain why an S corporation is the featured attraction in this chapter.

The decision of whether to remain a C corporation or make the S corporation election is difficult for some businesses, but not so for counseling. The business of counseling is within the IRS definition of a "personal service corporation" that is "engaged in the performance of services in the fields of health . . . or consulting and at least 95 percent of the value of its stock is held by employees or their estates and beneficiaries."[11] As an owner and employee of an incorporated counseling business, that would make the C corporation a personal service corporation. So what's the big deal? A flat 34 percent tax on every dollar of taxable income, that's what! Can your new business, which is barely making enough to survive and pay you a small income, handle such a big tax bite? Not for long.

Faced with the maximum rate for personal service corporations, an S corporation is the only viable choice for many counseling businesses. By making the S corporation election, a counseling business can enjoy noticeable tax relief. However, all shareholders must agree to the status change. To be eligible for S corporation status, your business must be a domestic corporation with only one class of stock and no more than thirty-five shareholders. These shareholders can be individuals, estates, or certain types of trusts (partnerships and other corporations cannot be shareholders.), and each shareholder must be a citizen or resident of the United States. Nonresident aliens may not hold S corporation shares. All these requirements must be fulfilled to qualify for the S corporation election. There are more details on how to define these rules further; consult your accountant on all aspects of this business decision.

Depending on tax rules in effect at the time, the S corporation status may be intentionally terminated. However, under current rules you had best be sure that is really what you want since you must wait five years to restore the S corporation election.

NONPROFIT CORPORATIONS

The most critical point to remember is that your church-linked counseling center does not become a tax-exempt nonprofit corporation until the IRS says it does! And that approval occurs by filing the necessary requests in addition to the corporate charter and other organizational processes. Carefully review the information in IRS Publication 557, *Tax-Exempt Status for Your Organization.* Failure to handle this process properly results in major tax problems, not to mention the nightmare of a public disgrace for soliciting donations to an organization that is not properly approved to do so. Without this approval the tax deductions claimed by your donors can be disallowed. This will cause them to lose their tax deductions, and they will be forced to pay additional taxes plus interest and penalties. Donors essentially rely on your assurance that your organization has tax-exempt status. If these warnings sound harsh, it is because the consequences are devastating. When ministries fall due to incompetence, fraud, or mismanagement, every organization in the body of Christ suffers.

The process and forms used in gaining IRS approval for tax-exempt status are discussed in Chapter 4. As noted in that chapter, tax-exempt organizations must apply for an employer identification number (EIN) on Form SS-4. Note also that a tax-exempt organization must still file employment tax returns.

The tax-exempt status does not eliminate any obligations as an employer. Even a tax-exempt organization that "pays wages to employees is responsible for withholding, depositing, paying and reporting federal income tax, social security taxes (FICA) and federal unemployment tax (FUTA) for such payments."[12] There are some exceptions, including the elected exemption from FICA tax for churches or church-controlled organizations under Form 8274, *Certification by Churches and Qualified Church-Controlled Organizations Electing Exemption From Employer Social Security Taxes*.[13] Do not just assume your organization fits the IRS definition of a qualified church-controlled organization; compare your situation with the information contained in Publication 557 and consult your accountant.

An important issue raised in Form 1023 is about sources of income. Question 11 in Part II asks if recipients of the organization's services are required to pay for services received. Here is where the subject of counseling fees and services must be clearly explained. You have to describe the benefits, services, or products that are offered and attach a copy of your current fee schedule. If a sliding scale is used, show how this is applied by income levels, state-assistance-recipient categories, or some other method. Also you are asked if any services are limited to specific individuals or classes of individuals and how those recipients are selected.[14] These questions will already be answered if you invested adequate time in formulating a business plan. If not, then the IRS is doing you a favor by forcing you to address these important operational issues.

As an approved 501(c)(3) tax-exempt organization, your counseling center files Form 990, *Return of Organization Exempt From Income Tax* or the Short Form 990-EZ. Specific rules related to the filing, explanations on how to complete the forms, and blank copies of these forms are found in IRS Package 990. This package also includes information on the potentially thorny problem of unrelated business income. This involves regular business income that is not substantially related to the purpose for which tax-exempt status was given. All unrelated business income in excess of $1,000 is subject to tax. For more information, see IRS Publication 598, *Tax on Unrelated Business*

Income of Exempt Organizations. As a safety precaution, before you begin any new venture within your tax-exempt organization, discuss it with your accountant and attorney to avoid the problems of unrelated business income.

Nonprofit organizations are formed to serve a need; they render services to benefit designated recipients. And as you know, to give aid in the name of the Lord is to give the service directly to Him. The counselor-administrator and employees in a nonprofit corporation can be paid for their work; however, due to the mission-directed (versus profit-directed) nature of these corporations, the workers are often paid less than comparable positions in for-profit corporations. The exemptions given to qualified 501(c)(3) organizations are a great example of mutual back-scratching because exemptions benefit the organization by eliminating the tax burden, which in turn extends its resources so that the organization continues to serve unmet needs in the community.

A Closing Comment

Law and accounting libraries are filled with explanations, cases, and rulings on the subjects presented in this chapter. Due to space limitations, these business tax issues are presented in broad terms featuring the key concepts. Also, this book is for counselors and ministers who have minimal knowledge of accounting or tax law. The intent is to acquaint you with important terminology, basic requirements, and sources of reference information. References were chosen from free, consumer-oriented IRS publications to encourage you to read on tax questions that pertain to your business. Further citations to the tax code and tax court rulings can be found in these publications, which present information in language that a non-CPA can understand easily. To order any IRS publication or tax form mentioned, call 1-800-829-3676. (See Appendix A for additional information on how to order the resources noted in this chapter.)

The information on business tax issues is given to educate and motivate you to work closely with your professional tax and legal advisers. It is not intended to be a substitute for accounting, legal, or tax advice rendered by appropriate professionals on behalf of your situation.

NOTES

1. Helvering v. Gregory, 69f.2d 809, 810, 1934

2. *Tax Guide for Small Business*, Internal Revenue Service Publication 334 (revised November 1992).

3. *U.S. Master Tax Guide* (Chicago: Commerce Clearing House, 1993).

4. *Tax Guide for Small Business*, 6.

5. Ibid., p. 8

6. Ibid.

7. *Employment Taxes and Information Returns*, Internal Revenue Service Publication 937 (1992), 4.

8. Ibid., 18.

9. Letter to Geriatric Support Programs from the Internal Revenue Service, 6 November 1992.

10. *Tax Guide for Small Business*, 115

11. Ibid., 124.

12. *Tax-Exempt Status for Your Organization*, Internal Revenue Service Publication 557 (revised January 1992), 9.

13. Ibid.

14. Internal Revenue Service Form 1023 (revised September 1990).

Chapter Ten

Business Ethics for Counseling

A good name is more desirable than great riches.

Proverbs 22:1

In the classic sense, ethics is the principle of moral conduct that influences a person's behavior. A written code of ethics sets the standards for practice and rules that govern members of a professional group. Even in our morally bankrupt society, clients want to know that their counselor operates on a higher standard of conduct. Fortunately for Christian counselors, we already have the highest standard of ethics modeled by Christ during His public ministry on earth. As we counsel and manage our businesses according to scriptural principles, we are able to meet and exceed any professional code of ethics.

Professional Credibility

A can of green peas requires a detailed nutritional label to explain what the buyer is getting. Yet a consumer entrusts his or her deepest secrets and problems to a counselor whose qualifications may not be as clearly presented as the contents on that can of green peas. It is no wonder consumers of counseling services are easily confused, because even in states with strict licensure laws, the title *counselor* is loosely appropriated by persons who do not meet any legal or reporting standards.

If you achieve and maintain a high level of training, do not be shy about admitting it. Informing clients about your training, license, or other credentials is appropriate disclosure prior to the beginning of the therapeutic relationship. An important aspect of the counselor-client interaction is that the client believes you have the skills and ability to help him or her; thus, providing information that substantiates your professional credibility will ease the client's unspoken concerns about choosing a competent counselor.

LICENSURE AND CERTIFICATION

Earning a license or certification for practice shows that you have met rigorous standards of education and supervised training under qualified practitioners. Your counseling knowledge has been tested both on paper and in actual client sessions. To sustain that license or certification, continuing education courses and compliance with laws and codes of ethic are required.

Each state government has a department that is charged with the regulation of the healthcare profession. From your state's regulatory agency, you can obtain copies of the existing state statutes on counseling practice. Even if you are not licensed or planning to be licensed, it is a good idea to review your state laws to determine whether you can legally continue the work that you are doing without a license or supervision. My state, Florida, is so concerned about the potential abuses that occur when untrained counselors treat clients with serious emotional problems that a special toll-free hotline is now open just to report unlicensed practitioners. Many other states deal just as severely with unlicensed practitioners, even those who try to argue that they are exempt from regulation as pastoral counselors. Some states have *practice acts* that regulate the practice of mental health counseling and specify what therapeutic modalities may be used. These regulations were developed to hold counselors accountable for what they do (or fail to do), not to quibble over their title. A mandatory practice act has far sharper legal teeth than a voluntary practice act.

While there is still ample room for true pastoral counseling, when such work drifts into the realm of mental health counseling without efforts to refer or seek consultation, ministers create dangerous liability situations for themselves and their churches. Just one case can generate enough financial pressure to bankrupt a church and destroy a minister's career. The more pastoral counselors extend their work to problems that are defined by statute as within the practice of professional counseling, the more likely that pastoral counseling will be targeted for regulation in future years. Although ministers cannot always avoid being in a counseling situation that takes an unexpected turn, a wise minister will learn how to recognize that kind of situation and will prayerfully seek the right action to take from that point forward. In such instances a cooperative relationship between a minister and a Christian professional counselor can work by referral, consultation, or supervision to meet the legal responsibilities involved and to protect the client's best interests.

Admittedly, licensure is certainly not a foolproof means of legislating ethical practice. If you read your state's report of counselor disciplinary actions and suspension of licenses you will quickly realize that this is not a perfect system. Yet counselor license boards do carry a big economic stick in their power to suspend or revoke a counselor's license and put him or her out of business. Furthermore, license categories help the public to identify different levels of counseling practice such as Licensed Clinical Social Worker, Licensed Mental Health Counselor, Licensed Marriage and Family Therapist, Licensed Professional Counselor, and Clinical Psychologist. Although some overlap exists in various license categories (depending on state statutes), a consumer can receive information from the licensing board that defines the education and experience requirements for each type of license. Consumers can also call the state regulatory board to find out if a counselor holds a valid license. If you look closely at the preamble or opening text of any state counselor-licensing laws, you will find that their purpose is to protect the public by establishing minimum standards of education and training to practice counseling and by specifying ongoing continuing-education requirements for counselors to remain in practice. Without any type of regulation, the potential for harm to confused consumers is catastrophic.

Professional organizations issue certifications to individuals who meet and maintain well-defined standards of practice. Although certification requirements can be challenging, by pursuing certification you will make a significant investment in your career. Meaningful certifications require some or all of the following measures of achievement: attainment of a master's or doctor's degree from a regionally accredited institution, a minimum level of counseling experience, one or more years of supervised practice in a specialty area, additional postgraduate training, presentation of a counseling technique, written or recorded text of your counseling intervention, a passing grade earned on a written exam, and sponsorship by other certified professional counselors or hospital experience supervised by the psychiatric team leader. Difficult, yes. Time consuming, definitely. However, the only certifications worth having are those that are earned. If you can get a certification by merely filling out a form and paying a fee without any demonstration of professional competence, that certificate is not worth the paper on which it is printed. The title may sound official but it is just a con game. Steve Levicoff points out that counselors must be wary of sham organizations that purchase ads to promote their phony counseling credentials in major Christian publications.[1] Once news of a phony credential surfaces, the counselor will face embarrassment and possible penalties, particularly if the claims of expertise based on those credentials place him or her in violation of state counseling statutes.

Pursuing certification does take time away from your counseling practice, and in the early stages of building a new business, that is a price you probably cannot afford. So place certification among your personal goals for the second, third, or fourth year in business. Do not upset the priorities in your business plan just because you *lust after* a few extra initials beside your name. In reality, certification is not enough of a practice-builder to offset the loss of your core clients while you study for an exam or attend classes.

Certification is not a means around any state licensing law unless that law specifically recognizes the certification as equal. Some certifications are nationally recognized while others are limited to regional or organizational acknowledgment. Due to the cost of time and training, it makes sense to pursue the certification that relates to your primary area of practice and is the most widely accepted as a standard of excellence in that specialty.

EXPERIENCE

Some of the greatest lessons learned about counseling come from time spent in sessions with actual clients. Role-plays are great, but there is nothing like OJT (on-the-job training). In fact, that is why license and certification qualifications require supervised experience. Once he or she has completed the supervision stage, an effective counselor continues to grow professionally with new training and voluntary peer supervision. A specialty may also develop as you gain more and more referrals for marriage counseling or adolescent counseling from satisfied former clients, or when new clients seek you out because they have seen a meaningful change in their friends or family members. They want to benefit from your experience in working with clients who have overcome similar problems. From the man on the street to the ivy halls of academia, experience is respected.

While some counselors fear that talking about experience treads on confidentiality issues, there are ways to avoid this problem. For example, you may say that you have counseled more than one hundred couples with serious relationship disputes, or perhaps you can state that you have more than two thousand hours of testing and evaluation experience with hyperactive children. With some thought you can translate your counseling experience into measurable terms such as years of counseling practice or hours of group work that substantiate the time you have devoted to your profession. However, take care that you never round off to the nearest hundred hours or in any way distort your actual experience for promotional reasons.

As always, check the counselor laws in your state to find out if any type of experience disclosure is permitted in advertising or client information brochures. Many state statutes governing counseling also rule on acceptability of advertising, public comments, or any communication designed to attract clients. What is not allowed is any public testimony about your work or any discussion of case histories without prior written consent from the clients. Even if the client gives permission, you have a responsibility to consider whether or not revelation of this information may be detrimental to the client or the client's family.

EDUCATION

While continuing education is mandated for counselors who seek to renew their state license or certifications, it should be the ethical responsibility of all counselors: pastoral, paraprofessional, and professional. Learning new therapeutic techniques is part of the commitment to counseling. You will never know so much or practice so long that you are unable to benefit from fresh ideas and new approaches.

Without being faddish, counselors need to read research reports and keep current on the progress of the profession. Thanks to the mass media and its talk-show glorification of dysfunctional behaviors, your clients may hear the latest theory on television before you have time to read it in a journal. Along this same line, you need to be aware of how pop psychology influences many of your clients and therefore sabotages your therapeutic efforts. When that happens, you have to do some reeducation of your client as part of the counseling. A quick way to familiarize yourself with the current psycho-trends is to scan the lead articles that adorn the covers of popular magazines at your local newsstand. In less than twenty minutes each month, you can become aware of the buzz words and new (or rehashed) theories to which your clients stubbornly cling. Since much of what a new client knows about counseling comes from mass media, counselors need to step into the client's frame of reference by applying this consumer's view technique.

In a more traditional framework, counselors must be lifelong learners. Subscribe to at least two respected journals and pledge to read six to twelve books each year that expand your current knowledge or introduce you to new techniques. This is not the kind of continuing education that someone else is monitoring, and it probably will not count as continuing education hours, yet what value can you place on the suicide intervention that you read about and then use successfully to persuade a man or woman to give life another chance? You deal with many people whose relationships and grip on reality are barely two steps away from the edge. Every skill, every technique, and every intervention you learn gives you greater resources to draw upon when you face a complex counseling situation. Scripture reminds us that "wise men store up knowledge" (Prov. 10:14). That is why you must budget your time (see chapter 7) weekly or bi-monthly for continuing education, conferences, or other professional-development activities that enhance your competence to counsel.

PERSONAL CREDIBILITY

In counseling, as in other fields, the operation of a business reflects the personal character of the leader. Business is never value-neutral. Thus in a counseling practice, the personal credibility of the counselor-administrator is a significant factor in the reputation of the practice. We want the secular community to know we are Christians by our exemplary behavior in the conduct of business. That means no shades of gray are acceptable. And there will be no shades or shadows when your counseling business operates in the Light!

HONEST ACCOUNTING

Business accounting must always be current, accurate, and ready for audit. When mistakes are discovered, they need to be dealt with promptly and compensation made for any inequities. More than likely, these are bookkeeping errors that are found by your accountant, or mistakes that are the result of inexperience, not fraud. Naturally, as the business grows and the counselor-administrator matures in the management role, bookkeeping errors can be expected to decrease. Now while columns of numbers are fairly straightforward, other types of recordkeeping and accounting related to counseling can appear to be more subjective. Let us review these so-called subjective issues under the light of scriptural ethics.

Insurance billing is an area in which the application of loose ethics can become a matter of fraud that is subject to serious punishment. The gray areas generally have to do with unwarranted flexibility in the interest of getting paid. For example, let us assume that a counselor treats a client with a personality disorder who is also feeling depressed over the complications and broken relationships that can be attributed to this disorder. The counselor knows that a certain insurance company or employee assistance program does not pay for treatment of personality disorders, but the client cannot afford the full cost of treatment. So treading the gray line, the counselor diagnoses the depression and conveniently ignores the personality disorder. This method of *selective diagnosis* may not be entirely incorrect—but neither is it totally honest.

Another kind of misrepresentation occurs when a counselor alternates two or three *pet diagnoses* or treatment categories into which clients are placed. While this one-size-fits-all diagnostic method is easy for the counselor, it is also potentially libelous when the pet diagnosis misses the mark by a country mile. Then there is *diagnosis du jour* (diagnosis of the day) based on what treatment is paying the best reimbursement for the longest period of time. Another gray area is the *twofer diagnosis*, designed to get two people into therapy for the price of one. The catch is that the insurance company is being billed for only one client—the one who has insurance coverage. This pathetic ploy is commonly used to get reimbursement for marriage counseling when the insurer does not cover such treatment. Marriage problems often result in some feelings of anxiety, depression, or adjustment, so the counselor makes a giant leap into the closest related diagnosis that will pay (any of the three just mentioned are commonly used). Not only is this dishonest with regard to the treatment that is actually given, but it may result in an unhappy surprise for the identified client. He or she is labeled with a diagnosis that may cause future problems in gaining employment in high-security industries or may restrict the opportunity to become licensed in some professions. Some mental health diagnoses are considered lifestyle risk factors similar to smoking, obesity, and sedentary occupations.

Major insurance companies are aware of these *games* and conduct periodic audits to seek out offenders. With sophisticated computer analyses, insurers can identify repeated bills for the same diagnosis, repeated use of the same number of sessions for treating a problem, or other *coincidences* that bear further investigation. For example, if you are a specialist in phobias and demonstrate that the majority of your clients, both those who pay privately and those who get insurance reimbursement, seek counseling for this problem then you have a strong case for billing the same diagnosis. However, if you are trying to *pull a fast one*, know that insurance company mental health case reviewers have seen this game before. Any type of fraudulent billing or deception designed to gain reimbursement is dealt with severely under state laws. If the insurance company is outside your state or represents Medicare, Champus, or Medicaid, investigation and prosecution may be initiated at the federal level.

Perhaps you share my amazement at the justifications used to support these methods of dishonest accounting. The winner in the repression category is the faulty belief that "the client gets treatment anyway and is not harmed by a little change of diagnosis." The second runner-up in the irrational excuse division is "just ask three therapists to make a diagnosis and you get three different opinions, so who is to say this diagnosis is wrong and theirs is right?" The book of Proverbs gives many examples of ethical versus unethical business dealings and reminds us that "the LORD abhors dishonest scales, but accurate weights are his delight" (Prov. 11:1). A counselor controls the *scales* or the ability to give a diagnostic label. Only "accurate weights" or appropriate application of a diagnosis is legally and ethically acceptable for Christian counselors.

FAIRNESS TOWARD EMPLOYEES

In your private practice or church-linked ministry, you are likely to have some experience in selecting and managing employees. Another of your many hats is that of "human resources specialist." It would seem that a counselor trained in empathy, conflict resolution, and fair confrontation would have an advantage over other business managers, but, unfortunately, reality does not bear witness to that assumption. Just as the shoemaker's children are the last to get shoes, the counselor's employees may be treated with less concern than that lavished on clients.

And ignorance of personnel management simply is no excuse! Laws that mandate certain minimum work standards exist to guide the employer and protect the employee. When the counselor-administrator uses service to the Lord as an excuse to support his or her workaholic beliefs, the same out-of-balance lifestyle may be expected of employees. This is a situation in which guilt becomes the inducement that violates standards set by the state's wage and hour board. Then there are the so-called independent contractors who really do not qualify for that status (see chapter 9). Under the guise of saving money, an employer tries to get the employee to work as an independent contractor to avoid paying taxes, worker's compensation, or other benefits. In researching this book, several examples were given to me of ministry boards and churches who take this approach. Yet shortchanging employees to have more money available for ministry is a distortion of the very concept of ministry. There is no scriptural support for miserly means as justification for a righteous result.

"The man of integrity walks securely, but he who takes crooked paths will be found out" (Prov. 10:9). Public image aside, your employees know you as you really are. If you are shading the gray, they will know it. If you speak about love and Christian values in the workplace, yet allow gossip and discrimination to fester between co-workers, your employees will be the first to see the hypocrisy. The attitudes with which you handle daily business operations reveal whether you sincerely trust in the Lord or lean on your own flawed judgments.

DEPENDABILITY

Counseling demands a servant's heart and a willingness to be available to minister as needed. Clients rely on you to keep appointments and to devote your full attention to them during each session. How will they know if you are being intentionally quiet and analytical or verbalizing an occasional "uh-huh" when you are really daydreaming about your upcoming vacation? Clients rely on the counselor's ability to be fully present in each session.

Your clients also depend upon your willingness to accept your own limitations. If a case exceeds your skills, you have an ethical responsibility to refer the client elsewhere or seek consultation. Clients rarely know when you are out of your skill range. They give you their trust and expect to receive help and hope. If you delay referral because of monetary gain or pride, you inflict harm on your client. That is a serious violation of the client's trust.

If you accept a client with severe emotional traumas or chronic disorders, never offer to be available in the next crisis time unless you really mean it. Handing a client half of a lifeline is no help at all. When you agree to allow a client to contact you for crisis stabilization, you must be available by pager or through your answering service. During your vacation or other absences, you need to arrange for a qualified therapist to take your emergency calls. Failure to provide alternative care for your most needy clients is abandonment, and that is a serious liability problem.[2] If your fervent prayer is "Lord deliver me from borderlines and other personality disorders who ring my phone in the night," then you have an ethical obligation to refer these clients to another therapist. Never accept or continue with a client whose needs are beyond your ability or patience to treat.

"All hard work brings a profit, but mere talk leads only to poverty" (Prov. 14:23). Counselors become known in the community for their dependability and their work ethic. Even clients who are far from being emotionally healthy can recognize and praise your willingness to *be there* for them. And clients who have successfully overcome their problems with your help will tell others about your faithfulness and patience. In this service business you need a servant's heart. And that is what will make your practice prosper: dependability and steadfast application of Christian principles in your business operation and in counseling with clients.

CONFIDENTIALITY

Counselors hear the cries of wounded people and the most painful family secrets. Clearing out the emotional garbage is part of the therapeutic process. But clients need to feel safe with you before they can make these difficult disclosures. To protect the client, state laws and counselor codes of ethics affirm the right of confidentiality and stipulate the terms under which it can be broken. "A fool's mouth is his undoing, and his lips are a snare to his soul" (Prov. 18:7). As a counselor, you are expected to know how your state defines and guards confidentiality.

Many states have laws similar to the Florida statute on psychotherapist-patient privilege.[3] Under this law, confidential communication between therapist and client is not to be revealed to any third party without client approval or certain other conditions. Conditions for breaching confidentiality are basically situations that involve imminent danger to the client or other persons or by judicial order. For example, the claim of privileged communications does not apply when a child or an aged or disabled adult is being abused or neglected. Statutes generally define what types of activities constitute neglect, abuse, and exploitation. Mental health professionals are among a list of *mandatory reporters* who are legally and ethically bound to report any known abuse or reasonable cause to suspect abuse involving children, elders, or disabled adults. However, most state statutes also require that abuse on *any person* must be reported.

The requirement to report abuse creates a complex dilemma for pastors. Does a pastoral counselor claim the historic clergy-penitent privilege that evolved from the Catholic Church's seal of the confessional? Or is a pastoral counselor bound by existing state statute to report known or suspected abuse? Which is the moral choice, and which is the legally defensible choice? Which is right before God? Pastoral counselors who are not licensed under state counselor laws must make a detailed study of their responsibilities in consultation with an attorney. Do not wait for a volatile situation to occur. Know the limits of pastoral confidentiality in your state.

Licensed professional counselors acting in their role as counselors are bound by state laws on confidentiality and by duty to report abuse. The state statutes that were in operation at the time of your license exam are subject to changes, so for the sake of legal protection keep up-to-date on any revisions to the statutes on confidentiality. Also, read everything you see on the legal applications of your duty to report abuse and your duty to warn persons who may be in danger from violent actions by your client. The duty to warn is the outcome of the famous Tarasoff case[4] in which a young woman was killed by her jealous boyfriend who had communicated his malicious intentions to his therapist before the fatal attack. This case and subsequent related cases demonstrate that laws affecting the therapist-client relationship are continually subject to revision based on judicial rulings, legal challenges, and pressure for change brought on state legislatures.

On a less intense level, many violations of client confidentiality occur in nonmalicious, casual ways. If you apply to an insurance company for reimbursement, your client must agree to make (or allow you to make) the claim and be informed that diagnostic and other relevant case information is being transmitted to the insurer in order to obtain payment. Any time you obtain the client's signature authorizing you to file insurance claims, transmit case information to another therapist, or request medical information from a physician, be certain that your client is capable of giving *informed consent*. If your client is a minor, an adult under guardianship, or an adult whom you have reason to believe is not competent to give consent, then you must get the consent of a responsible party. Before acting on any situation that is questionable, consult your attorney. There are some exceptions for life-threatening emergencies that give you greater latitude to disclose information to a hospital or law-enforcement officer that may be necessary to stabilize or protect the client. Verify any such provisions according to your state laws.

Other violations of confidentiality that the counselor-administrator must carefully guard against include the accessibility of client records by support staff. A secretary who types insurance claim forms knows the client's name and diagnosis. Typing the counselor's treatment summary or copying treatment notes for an insurance company gives ample opportunity to sneak a peak. Suppose your secretary unintentionally tells a friend that Mrs. X is coming for counseling, or that she tries to help Mrs. X by submitting a poorly disguised prayer request to the church prayer group. These subtle breaches of confidentiality are *your responsibility*. As the counselor, you are accountable both legally and ethically. Before you allow your staff to handle any confidential information, you must inform them of the client's right to privacy and the serious consequences of breaching that confidentiality.

Dilemmas of confidentiality and pastoral privilege may be the most difficult ethical problems professional and pastoral counselors face. At times the questions of what to tell, who to tell, and when to tell it seem like moving targets, and it is a challenge to keep up with the changes brought by legal actions. So if you read only one article in the many journals that crowd your mailbox, read the one on confidentiality and counselors' legal responsibilities. This thorny issue is definitely a lawsuit maker and a career breaker.

Dual Relationships

The increasing instances of trouble with dual relationships may soon eclipse violations of confidentiality as the leading problem in the therapeutic alliance. A dual relationship involves the therapist's intent to engage in two or more different types of relationships with a client. In keeping with the highest clinical standards, the therapeutic relationship does not mix with familial, romantic, sexual, political, or business relationships. The purpose of this strict limitation is so that the client relates to the therapist on one level only. The counseling room needs to be a safe haven in which a client is assured of receiving the therapist's respect, attention, and highest level of care. That is a true therapeutic environment—anything less is a sham and potentially harmful to the client.

If the therapist and client are involved in a real estate transaction or are in-laws by marriage, the therapeutic relationship is continually affected by the outside relationship. Neither client nor therapist can totally remove any considerations of these other connections from the therapy session.

Perhaps the most heinous violations of the therapeutic relationship occur when a romantic or sexual relationship is allowed to develop between therapist and client. "Like a city whose walls are broken down is a man who lacks self-control" (Prov. 25:28). State laws and codes of ethics strictly forbid sexual relationships between a counselor and counselee. The severity of the sexual or romantic dual relationship is compounded by the unbalanced roles involved. Some states have laws similar to that of the Florida statute that clearly states that the

> effects of the psychotherapist-client relationship are powerful and subtle, and that clients are influenced consciously and subconsciously by the unequal distribution of power inherent in such relationships . . . the client should be irrebuttably presumed incapable of giving valid, informed, free consent to sexual activity involving the psychotherapist.[5]

Penalties for sexual misconduct, both verbal and physical, include fines, censure, or loss of license to practice. As severe as the penalties are, they seem almost inadequate punishment for the emotional damage done to the client.

Sometimes counselors and pastors unwittingly become the object of a client's fantasies or misplaced affection. The real test of personal integrity is in how these situations are identified, confronted, and managed. Scriptural admonitions about yielding to temptations of the flesh apply as if they were written specifically to guard against aberrations in the therapist-client relationship.

Other less volatile situations involving dual relationships can be less obvious yet equally dangerous. University professors are wrestling with their concerns that being both a clinical supervisor and a professor for a student is a dual relationship. Church counseling centers wonder if it is acceptable to hire a recent counseling graduate who, during a troubled adolescence, was a client of the center. Can you accept your pastor's referral to counsel a person who is in your Sunday school class? Is it possible to develop a friendship with a counselor under your supervision? These are all complex questions. You need to review any and all provisions of your state statutes that deal with dual relationships. Additional guidance can be obtained from codes of ethics and standards of practice issued by professional counselor organizations and pastoral associations. If you are also an ordained pastor, consult with your denominational leadership for advice or rulings on the dual relationship issue. As with confidentiality, the rulings that involve dual relationships are continuing to evolve.

Implement a three-point program to protect yourself and your clients: (1) Stay informed of cases and rulings on this problem; (2) Schedule regular peer supervision in which you can discuss potential problems; and (3) Submit your thoughts and actions to scriptural verification. If you do, you will have the spiritual strength to recognize and rebuke temptations to engage in dual relationships.

Lifestyle

The lifestyle of a Christian is a testimony more powerful than the most eloquent words. To declare yourself a Christian counselor is to open your life for scrutiny. Clients want to know if you just "talk the walk" or if you really "walk the walk." You may be able to put up a righteous front at your office, but what about other places in the community where you are seen? Clients notice how you dress and behave in public places. And just as revealing is the kind of public places where you are seen. A substance-abuse counselor who frequents a local bar or a family counselor who is overheard screaming insults to his or her children displays a lifestyle message that contradicts the desired image of a Christian counselor.

"When a man's ways are pleasing to the LORD, he makes even his enemies live at peace with him" (Prov. 16:7). God knows your heart and your motivations. He will bless your work that is done humbly in His name and in a right spirit. That is the essence of my personal theme for counseling: "God is the healer. I am merely the helper." Setting aside the human desire to praise your own efforts, "commit to the LORD whatever you do, and your plans will succeed" (Prov. 16:3). Even non-Christian clients who disagree with your spiritual beliefs can respect you for adhering to those beliefs. Christians who come to you for counseling expect to find that biblical truth is a part of their therapy. If you hold yourself out to be a Christian counselor and fail to show any reliance on scriptural principles, you are on a self-destructive course. Better to be a competent secular counselor than a Christian counselor in name only. God is not mocked, and, frankly, your clients will not take kindly to being hoodwinked.

Church Involvement

The local church is home base for the believer; it is our center of worship, family activities, fellowship, and spiritual renewal. Christian counselors need to be involved in a local church. And involved does not mean present occasionally or only visible when called to teach. Those of us who are called to counsel in the name of the Lord need the regular renewal that is found only in a strong Bible-teaching church.

Clients often want to know what church you attend and what is your testimony. Very rarely are they concerned with which denomination you belong to as much as they want to know that you are faithful in your church commitment. When pastors from other churches ask similar questions about your spiritual background, you can also say, "You are welcome to call my pastor to inquire about my lifestyle and my commitment to our church." True, we are not saved by our works, but we do have a faith that works in all aspects of life. The Lord expects us to demonstrate a working faith by accepting our place of ministry within the local church.

"Blessed is the man who listens to me, watching daily at my doors, waiting at my doorway. For whoever finds me finds life and receives favor from the LORD" (Prov. 8:34–36). Pastors and Christian counselors must have a daily recharge from the Word of God to be able to give away their faith and their strength to others in need. To be so close to human suffering and satanic oppression demands an extra measure of spiritual strength that a counselor can only receive through regular prayer, Scripture reading, and maintaining a close walk with the Lord. Sometimes evening counseling appointments or crisis calls prevent counselors from attending services or special meetings as often as they would like. However, nothing prevents you from daily Bible study and prayer before and during your work day. If necessary, arrive at the office an hour before appointments begin to start your day in prayer. You cannot always attend every church service, but you can have praise and worship in your office, your car, or while taking an early-morning walk. The spiritual strength you gain from personal prayer and church involvement are the *manna* that sustains you as a counselor.

Legal Responsibilities

The subject of laws to govern counseling sparks debate among some Christian and pastoral counselors who claim that God is their only authority. Others acknowledge the right of a state to protect the health and welfare of its citizens, yet they fear future encroachment of the laws that might limit biblical counseling approaches. As always, Scripture brings balance to the issue.

> Remind the people to be subject to rulers and authorities, to be obedient, to be ready to do whatever is good, to slander no one, to be peaceable and considerate, and to show true humility toward all men. (Titus 3:1–2)

Following that advice keeps you in compliance with almost any law regulating ethical counseling practice.

State and Local Laws

As discussed in the beginning of this chapter, laws in many states are so strictly drawn that a license for practice is required in all but clearly pastoral duties. Even states with more lenient regulations are taking second looks at the higher standards for practice. Christian counselors must know the law and be in compliance as required.

In addition, municipalities and counties have laws that relate to the counseling business. For example, the city in which my office is located does not allow me to obtain an occupational license under the same professional category as my state license to practice. The city places licensed and unlicensed

counselors under the nebulous category of *consultant.* A clerk
at the city licensing office told me the city does not want to
issue any occupational licenses under *counselor* and risk giving credibility to someone who has not earned it.

Your counseling office or church-linked counseling center must
comply with local laws for obtaining occupational licenses. In
some municipalities, you are required to have both a city and
county occupational license. That is the case in my area. Yet to
save money, some counselors choose to purchase the cheaper occupational license and plead ignorance of anything more. My
county license is $15 and my city license is $70. However, since
my office location is governed by both city and county, both licenses are necessary. This is a small example of honesty in
business that we must display as Christian business managers.

If your county or municipality has any other laws relating
to your counseling practice, you have a responsibility to know
and comply with those laws. This is an important part of your
witness in the business community.

Codes of Ethics

The Christian and secular counselor organizations have
codes of ethics that detail what is considered ethical practice
for members. When you accept membership in or certification
from an organization, you are affirming your intent to follow
the prescribed code of ethics. If you do not, you face censure
and expulsion from the organization and withdrawal of your
certification.

Take time to read the code of ethics for any organization in
which you seek membership. Codes of ethics generally take a
position on the nature of the therapist-client relationship, the
proper uses of appraisal instruments, the humane standards
for research, the prohibition on dual relationships, the standards for private practice, and the appropriate conduct in the
consulting relationship. In addition to those positions, codes
of ethics for Christian counseling associations include a statement of faith and confirm the appropriate use of biblical
authority as an element in the counseling process.

Most organizations include their code of ethics in their new-
member packet. Review several of these statements as part of

your decision-making process before committing to membership in any Christian or secular organization. Here is a hint: Copies of several codes of ethics are stapled to the inside cover of my book of state statutes and rules for counseling. When you face an ethical question, look at every source of information available. A Bible occupies the space next to my law book. That combination brings to bear every law of God and man to help me make the right choices. Some well-defined examples of secular codes of ethics are those from the National Board of Certified Counselors, the American Counseling Association, and the American Psychological Association. For Christ-centered codes of ethics, review the positions of the Christian Association for Psychological Studies, the American Association of Pastoral Counselors, and the American Association of Christian Counselors.

NOTES

1. Steve Levicoff, "The Final Word," *Christian Counseling Today*, October 1993.

2. George Ohlschlager and Peter Mosgofian, *Law for the Christian Counselor* (Dallas: Word, Inc.: 1992), 189.

3. Florida Statute 90.503, Psychotherapist-Patient Privilege.

4. Tarasoff v. Regents of the University of California, 13 Cal. 3d 117, 118 Cal. Rptr. 129, 529 p.2d 551 (1974).

5. Florida Chapter 21CC-10.001, Sexual Misconduct in the Practice of Marriage and Family Therapy, Clinical Social Work, and Mental Health Counseling.

Chapter Eleven

Finding Referral Sources

A generous man will prosper; he who refreshes others will himself be refreshed.

Proverbs 11:25

Most of us like to hear the "inside story," hence the popularity of those tell-all magazines. We are even more anxious to know the inside information on those who provide service to ourselves and our families. If your infant is ill, don't you feel better about taking the baby to a pediatrician who is recommended by your neighbor who has reared seven children? When you face major surgery, you are likely to ask around the medical community looking for affirmations about the skill of the surgeon. Anyone who recommends a service provider is giving a referral that is taken to be a personal endorsement.

Professionals know that referrals are necessary yet difficult because they put their own reputations on the line when they recommend that their clients work with a counselor. Here is where you must demonstrate to other professionals that you are worthy of their referrals. To accomplish this you need to engage in a highly specialized aspect of marketing that involves networking with potential referral sources. The most effective way to meet other professionals is through personal contact. A referral source wants to feel confident about your ability and ethics before sending his or her clients to you. Because if the client is satisfied with your counseling services, the referral source will be praised, but if the client feels mistreated or ignored, that discontent is likely to extend to the referral source.

For Christians, making referrals outside our own group or congregation is often necessary yet perilous. Only the Lord knows for certain, but the workplace may be where you are best able to find out how that professional expresses his or her faith. My worst experience with a referral concerned a married Christian woman who was overwhelmed with depression due to several recent losses. Before coming to me for counseling, she read some secular self-help books and decided that having an affair would enhance her self-esteem, lift her depression, and therefore, improve her marriage. Fortunately, she was feeling just enough conviction about her faulty logic to delay acting on this sinful fantasy. Because of the intensity of her depression, she was referred from my office to a Christian physician for medical evaluation, but instead of being evaluated by the physician, she was seen by his new associate. The newcomer told her that having an affair might validate her as a woman, and if nobody got hurt it might be just what she needed to relieve her depression! Imagine my righteous indignation upon hearing that report from my client. When confronted with this situation, the Christian physician made excuses for his associate and would not guarantee to personally treat my referral clients. As you can guess, no client from my office has since been referred to that physician!

Gaining the Attention of Referral Sources

As Scripture states, we are not "of the world" but we do function "in the world." This is also a business reality that Christian counselors have to accept in promoting their services to both Christian and secular referral sources. If you are a competent counselor who is willing to establish professional rapport for the benefit of your mutual client, secular professionals will refer their clients to you. This working relationship is an opportunity to show the unbeliever how much your work is enhanced by your Christianity. Demonstrate by your actions how you operate under God's work ethic: "Whatever you do, work at it with all your heart, as working for the Lord, not for men, since you know that you will receive an inheritance from the Lord as a reward" (Col. 3:23–24).

PRESENTING YOUR QUALIFICATIONS

Draft a one-page abridged résumé to give to referral sources. Keep it concise with plenty of margin space for easy reading and use bullets or bold type to draw attention to key information. Busy professionals do not have time to read your full curriculum vitae, so if you have experience in an area of interest to that referral source, highlight it early in the presentation.

Another way to present your qualifications is in a brochure. Use the six-panel format presented in chapter 6: Panel 1, your mission statement and types of counseling or testing offered; Panel 2, licenses, certifications, education; Panel 3, related experience or training; Panel 4, a brief practice history and a map to your office; Panel 5, a list of several references from respected professionals with a positive comment about you from each; and Panel 6, the cover featuring your name, address, telephone, and photo. Adding a photo personalizes the brochure and helps the referral source remember who you are. However, you will need to have these done by a printer to get a good-quality reprint of the photo. If you prefer to be more flexible in tailoring the copy, eliminate the cover photo. You can also purchase bordered paper designed for making brochures with your laser printer. By printing single copies you can easily make changes and still achieve a high-quality look.

Finding time for a personal meeting with busy referral sources can be difficult. Some professionals eat on the run during work hours and rarely leave the office for lunch. If you get resistance to a lunch invitation, ask the assistant or appointment secretary what other times are generally used for brief meetings. Early breakfast is a good way to get your referral source's full attention away from the office before interruptions and problems of the day interfere. Or ask if you can bring the snacks and meet with the professional during morning or afternoon coffee break. Remember that you are asking for free use of another person's time. Be brief, be informative, and be gone before overstaying your welcome.

Acknowledgment of Referrals

A referral is a vote of confidence in your counseling skills. As with any gift, an expression of gratitude to the giver is appropriate. If the referral comes with a request to consult periodically with the source (i.e., a physician monitoring medication wants a report on therapeutic progress), then affirm your understanding of the request in a letter. Otherwise, a handwritten or preprinted notecard serves the purpose. You can purchase attractive preprinted "thank you for the referral" cards with a standard or customized message (more expensive to print) from office supply stores and mail-order business stationery catalogs. Always sign (no stamp or preprint) your name and add a brief handwritten comment to someone you know well. Do not try to be too friendly too fast with a new professional contact.

Some generic referral cards have space for listing the name of the client; however, to maintain confidentiality this is not appropriate. Either use phrasing that merely says thank you for the referral or enter a nonidentifying description such as "the couple for marriage counseling" or the "individual for counseling." If your acknowledgment arrives promptly, the referral source generally knows who the client is. Is it ever acceptable to acknowledge a referral from a former client? Yes, as long as the response is very general such as, "Thank you for expressing your confidence in me by referring a new client."

Regular Correspondence

You want to keep referral sources aware of your work, but you must do that without overwhelming them with more junk mail. The old technique of sending generalized or self-aggrandizing monthly letters to lists of every physician, dentist, and attorney in the area is desperation marketing—and it is an expensive waste. Target your referral contacts into two groups:

those who periodically refer clients and those you are actively prospecting. Send different correspondence to active referral sources than to referral prospects.

If you publish a newsletter, send it to both sources and prospects. Otherwise, your primary goal in correspondence and meetings with prospects is to persuade them to give you a referral. You are still selling yourself as a competent counselor. With current sources who are already satisfied with your work, you want to continually affirm their trust in your skills. A great technique learned from my father is to keep notes on a card file of each source's professional and personal interests. Then anytime you see a journal or newspaper article about a subject of interest to that person, clip and send it. You might mail a story touting how counseling helps a client cope with medical treatment or a newspaper article on a new high-performance walking shoe to the physician-race walker. Attach your business card with a handwritten note saying, "I think you will be interested in this article." This small gesture of thoughtfulness shows that you think of the source as an individual and not just as someone who can do something for you. Of course you do not want to flood the source with trivial articles every month or your effort will lose its impact. Another idea is to clip news articles featuring a professional achievement or a quote by a referral source or prospect. Mail it in your personal notecard with a brief handwritten message of congratulations or other appropriate comment.

SHARE INFORMATION

You want to provide referral sources with supplemental information that supports the value of counseling and demonstrates that you keep up to date with new developments in your field. Here are a few easy ways to share information with other professionals. When you hear about an innovative therapy in a continuing-education lecture, type a summary of the comments and copy any handouts or bibliography and mail the package to selected referral sources. Have you purchased a cassette or video tape of a conference lecture you particularly enjoyed? Offer to lend it to your referral source. If you have written a journal article or paper on a counseling topic, send a copy to your referral source. When a special lecture on a topic of interest to your referral source is given at a counselor's meeting or local hospital, invite him or her to attend as your guest. Be sure to share only the information that is meaningful to each referral source.

Consultation

Let your referral source know that you are available for consultation in areas of your expertise. Such consultations are usually of limited duration on specific cases. Also, inform your referral sources about the types of testing and assessments you are qualified by license or training to perform and how such an evaluation can be useful to the referral source in working with his or her clients. For example, tell a surgeon about the value of identifying and teaching coping skills to an anxiety-prone patient before major surgery. Or explain to an attorney how much more effective the client can be as a witness by learning relaxation and stress-reduction techniques. Providing consultation to referral sources can take the form of direct client contact or indirect impact on the client by teaching or advising the professional who is in direct contact with the client.

Fairness, Not Equality, Prevails

Referrals are not an equal-opportunity situation. You may obtain a dozen referrals from one source before you can reciprocate, and, conversely, you may refer to other professionals without getting immediate or equal referrals in return. Accept the fact that your sources are being approached by other counselors. These sources have the same obligation that you do to recommend treatment from the most qualified providers who can best meet the client's needs. If you refer only to one favorite physician or attorney (who is also your golf or tennis buddy), this may become an issue of friendly nepotism versus ethics. On the other hand, if a referral source takes your information, calls you for advice, and then continually sends clients to another counselor, it is time to get the message that this source is not interested in referring to you. Equality is not always possible . . . fairness is.

WHERE TO FIND REFERRAL SOURCES

MEDICAL COMMUNITY

While healthcare providers direct their attention toward treatment that supports the mind-body connection, Christian healthcare providers go one step further to treat the whole person: mind, body, and spirit. Although you may prefer to work with Christians in the medical community, the patients of both Christian and secular providers can benefit from your counseling services.

Dentists and physicians are inundated with requests for referrals from almost every kind of healthcare service. So it is important that your referral-prospecting efforts stand out from the crowd. Stay with the targeted, personalized approaches previously discussed. Ask the physicians and dentists you already know to introduce you to their peers or recommend that you speak at a local professional meeting. After you work successfully with a client, request that the doctor write a letter affirming that your counseling skills supported medical or dental treatment. With the doctor's permission, present that recommendation letter to other professionals. A physician or dentist is more inclined to make the first referral to you based on substantiation of your skills by a fellow professional.

Chiropractors, licensed massage therapists, and physical therapists engage in direct client services just as you do in counseling. Due to the amount of time spent with clients during treatment, clients often tell these providers about the emotional as well as physical stresses in their lives. Talk with the provider or the office assistant about the types of clients and physical conditions that he or she typically treats. Make your presentation based on how the counseling techniques you use can help these clients cope with treatment, reframe negative thinking, focus attention, process trauma, or manage pain.

Many counselors fail to present their services to hospitals, assuming that these facilities already have complete mental health teams. However, many of the team members only work within the hospital. After discharge, the patient is often referred to a counseling center or private-practice therapist for follow-up psychotherapy. If you have the appropriate credentials and state license, you can become part of the hospital's referral network. Start by talking with the hospital social worker and other psychiatric program staff members. These people know which patients are about to be released and need to continue therapy. Some hospitals have a Christian "track" or specialized program to bring the spiritual element into treatment. Let the hospital program director and counseling staff know about your services. Even secular psychiatrists will refer to qualified Christian counselors when the patient desires to continue Christ-centered therapy after discharge.

Community Agencies

The larger your community, the greater the potential for referrals from both public and private agencies. A list of these services is often available at the chamber of commerce, the public library, the local newspaper, or the local government public affairs office. In my area, a joint-venture organization of several agencies produces and sells a directory of community resources. Before you approach any agency, find out about the types of service provided, the demographics of eligible clients, the source of its funding, and the name of the key person to contact.

Most state and local mental health agencies are overburdened with client loads that result in long waiting lists for treatment. These agencies may make referrals for clients requesting a Christian counselor if your counseling center offers sliding-scale fees or if you are a qualified Medicare or Medicaid provider. Another motivation for referral is when you provide highly specialized counseling such as for spouse abuse, sexual abuse, or predivorce mediation.

The growing number of single-parent families and two parents who rely on dual incomes is a boom for the day-care business. Day-care workers know a lot about family situations due to their frequent interactions with parents and children. Talk with the day-care center director about the services you can provide for assessment, family counseling, and parenting groups. If you are qualified, offer to conduct testing at the day-care center to determine the strengths and weaknesses of each child who is nearing entry to kindergarten. Many working parents gratefully accept testing and evaluations as a convenience; plus, the endorsement of the day-care center can be a regular source of new clients both for testing and subsequent family counseling.

Dieting is close to replacing baseball as America's national pastime. Catering to that demand for thinness at any price are a variety of medical and commercial diet programs. In many instances the *counseling* given to diet clients is a mixture of pep talk, sales pitch, and sympathy delivered by a person without any academic training in counseling or psychotherapy. Medically supervised programs usually have a nurse functioning as a program counselor, however, both medical and commercial diet programs may overlook the severe emotional connections to diet sabotage. Your counseling experience with eating disorders, bulimia, sexual abuse, and other traumas can help resistant diet clients improve their success rates by dealing with the underlying cause of overeating. Discuss how your individual or group counseling can support the client's desire for weight loss and offer to teach a session on behavior modification or self-esteem to a diet program group meetings.

Your County Extension Service is a hidden treasure of consumer information, special programs, and activities for all ages. In my area, the County Extension Service teaches classes, speaks to community groups, produces a television show on public access cable channel, sponsors 4-H for children and teens, and has a staff of in-house experts to deal with agricultural and consumer questions. Look over the services offered in your county and take note of what you can offer to supplement these consumer-oriented programs for families and children. Here is an example. For the last two years, the County Extension Service has recruited me to teach a session on behavior management in its weight loss and nutrition programs presented at local businesses. It is an opportunity for me to give my time in a community service program and to speak to prospective clients.

Peer support groups fill an important niche beyond what the healthcare system or other governmental agencies serve. This old-fashioned idea of people helping people is active in dealing with many issues from addictions to diseases to parenting. Some groups are affiliated with a national support organization while others are locally controlled. In reviewing the support groups in your area, identify those that match your counseling expertise. Contact the support group leader and offer to speak, share research information, or host the group at your office. Tell the leader how your counseling services can best be matched with the needs of the group. Some support groups have one or more professional advisers. This is extra work for you; however, it is another opportunity to contribute your time and talent as a community service while promoting your business.

Education Community

A college or university campus in your area is a treasure of research data, innovative programs, and potential referrals. The typical campus counseling center is under such a high demand for services that counseling is often short-term. More intensive treatment, or dealing with specialized issues, may be referred to other counselors or centers in the community. If you are an alumnus (or know someone who is), use that as your means of initiating contact with the director of the campus counseling center to discuss the types of services you can provide to students. Offer to conduct a limited-duration counseling group on campus. You can also agree to serve as a consultant to the counseling center staff in areas of your expertise.

Also introduce yourself to Christian student organizations. Christian students who are away from their families and their home church may languish in emotional pain rather than seek help at a secular campus counseling center. These students need you! Let them know about your services and other college-oriented programs at local churches. The word-of-mouth network among these students is a strong referral base.

Develop rapport with the psychology faculty. Some of these professors are licensed psychologists or mental health counselors who also staff the campus counseling center. Others are more involved in experimental psychology and less in people contact. However, these professors and associates know how to recognize students in emotional distress. Even if they are not trained in psychotherapy, students frequently assume that any psychology professor is a good counselor. After first introducing yourself to the department head, ask for his or her permission to briefly present your counseling services at the next faculty meeting. If that is not possible, meet each professor individually. Also express your willingness to speak to a class, demonstrate a technique, or allow students to contact you for career advice. Your services are usually even more welcome when you make them known to the faculty of a Christian college. These professors want their students to know practitioners of effective Christian counseling in the community as sources of encouragement and as role models.

Christian elementary and high schools struggle to provide high quality education at an affordable cost. Thus they cannot provide some of the specialized testing and evaluations funded through your tax dollars at public schools. Talk with the Christian school principal about counseling or testing services you can offer. If the school is large and the needs are great, you can agree to spend one day per week or two days monthly providing counseling to students at the school. In some schools, the principal and a teacher have already informed the parents that unless a child receives counseling, he or she will be dismissed. Principals also see many family problems that run much deeper than a child's behavior. Referring the family to a qualified Christian counselor transfers the focus out of the school and into family counseling, where all members of the family system can receive help.

Vocational-technical school teachers are very goal-directed toward helping students learn a skill and get a job as rapidly as possible. Often, financial pressures at home are behind these students' need to find employment. Public vo-tech schools have guidance counselors who focus on helping students select a program and find a job after graduation, but some private vo-tech schools are limited in programming and do not always have trained guidance counselors on staff. Also, these schools rarely have a counseling center as do most college campuses. You can provide a counseling center alternative. Meet with the director and faculty to inform them of your services for counseling and career testing and ask to place your brochures or flyers on student bulletin boards. Offer to speak to a class or conduct a limited group session on campus, but before you select a topic find out more about the demographics of the students. You may discover that there are both recent high school graduates and older single parents struggling to better support their children. Talk with faculty members about the concerns expressed by their students. Younger students can be more confused about career choices and how to handle job interviews, while older students are subject to more stress from balancing school and family as well as financial pressures. In the flyers distributed to students and in discussions with faculty, explain clearly how you can effectively work with both types of students in counseling. If you do not have a sliding fee scale, consider lowering the students' cost by offering groups. You will gain more referrals here if you make your service affordable to students on tight budgets.

Many communities have a displaced-homemakers program conducted at a local college, a junior college, or by a nonprofit organization. It is a sad commentary on our society's attitude about disposable marriages that many women in these programs are divorced or abandoned. Some women have taken their children and run for their lives to escape abuse. Other women in the program are widowed. All the women have been displaced or unexpectedly removed from their role as homemaker and thrust into the job market with little or no skills. Some well-funded programs have a full range of testing, counseling, and teaching. Others rely on resources and professionals in the community to supplement the program. If you have a heart for wounded women and their families, talk with the program director about your desire to be a community referral source. Due to financial constraints, many women in the program are living on limited support or public assistance, so if you are a Medicare or Medicaid provider, you will get more referrals. Otherwise, you can offer a sliding-scale fee or talk with the program director about being paid as an adjunct faculty member to conduct group or individual counseling that is not currently available.

Local Business and Industry

As medical insurance costs rise, businesses are trying to maintain a rocky balance between what employees want and what is affordable. A popular approach to this problem is to contract with employee assistance programs (EAP). Under contract to the business, EAPs give testing, evaluations, and counseling to employees. For cost control, the goal is usually to find the most effective short-term therapy. Since many EAPs are not large enough to have specialists on staff, when necessary, referrals are made to counselors in the community who will work under EAP review and for a predetermined fee. Before qualifying to receive referrals, you must complete an interview and screening process. When you talk with the EAP director, stating that you are a Christian counselor is an advantage. Several of my colleagues have gained referrals because the employee insisted on a Christian counselor. As long as you meet the educational and license qualifications required, you may be approved by the EAP as a Christian specialist.

Preferred provider organizations (PPOs) are similar to EAPs in that both are contracted to give services to employees of a business or industry. PPOs then contract with counselors in the community to render services at the counselors' offices. If you contract with a PPO, be specific about your specialties. Do not simply say "testing and assessments." Detail the types of testing by name and purpose. Regularly send an updated list of your group counseling topics and below each topic, give a brief paragraph explaining how this group addresses needs in the PPO client population. Propose to do a group exclusively for PPO clients on commonly seen issues such as career burnout, stress management, and midlife adjustment. The more cooperative you are to the PPO's needs and its paperwork demands, the more referrals you will receive.

Larger companies have a human resources staff that works closely with employees. This department also serves as an information center for job openings, employee benefits, and training programs. In dealing with employees on a personal level, human resources staff members may be the first to recognize symptoms of emotional distress related to job performance. If the company does not have a PPO or an EAP, referrals may be made directly to counselors in the community. Approach the human resources staff using similar ideas for presenting your services to PPOs and EAPs. Also ask a friend or church member who works in the company to contact or send a memo recommending your services to the human resources director.

In some industries, employee turnover is high due to lay-offs, seasonal contracts, or economic downturns. More and more large companies have outplacement coordinators who help employees transition back to school, move into the job market, or look for temporary work during layoffs. Think of the human needs in these situations: loss, grief, adjustment, anger, indecision, role changes, and stress to the individual and family. When you meet with outplacement coordinators, explain how your skills and services supplement their work with employees in transition. Ask the coordinators to include your brochure or group schedules in their outplacement information packets. You can also offer a group for families of workers in transition. This is a crying need that often is inadequately met.

Retirement issues are similar to those of transition, except that the change is permanent. Some very caring companies have a separate outplacement team to deal with retirement transition. Retirees experience the same emotional turmoil as transition workers, but they also have to cope with aging and reconciliation with self in the latter stages of life. Workers who have based their self-esteem in their work suddenly are left out in the cold. As baby boomers begin reaching retirement, the need for gerontological counseling is growing. If you have training to work with emotional problems of retirees, make known your expertise to the retirement transition team in local companies.

Christian Community

This is where we are at home in the fellowship of believers. Regardless of the denomination, pastors in your city want to know about qualified counselors whose work and testimony honors our Lord. Concerns about pastoral liability and levels of care place the church at increasing risk in certain counseling situations. Yet, pastors have a responsibility to care for their congregation. As a loving parent takes a child to a physician when conditions fail to respond to the best efforts at home and demand additional expertise, so, too, must pastors recognize severe emotional conditions that warrant referral to qualified Christian counselors. Knowing when to make referrals is part of the pastoral obligation, just as it is part of a counselor's duty to seek consultation or make referrals for conditions beyond his or her ability to treat. If your church and those near you do not have their own counseling centers, then you are doing a service for these pastors by informing them of your Christian counseling programs.

Begin by making your services available in your home church. Talk with the pastor about needs expressed in the congregation and offer low-cost, limited-duration counseling groups to address the most pressing needs. Sponsoring you to conduct groups at the church reinforces the members' link to the church. Whether the church pays your fee or allows you to charge a fee per person, the church members benefit. From those groups you often gain referrals for individual or family therapy.

Before approaching other pastors in your denomination, get a letter of recommendation from your pastor. This will be a valuable introduction particularly for those pastors who are more comfortable referring to counselors who share their denominational views. Offer to conduct groups at the church similar to that proposed for your home church.

Introducing your services to pastors in other denominations or independent churches requires some prior research into the beliefs of those churches. If their beliefs are compatible with yours, then a referral relationship is possible. However, when there are sharp denominational or scriptural interpretation conflicts, you are less likely to receive referrals. But do not exclude any nearby church. Faced with a choice of referring to an atheist or a Christian with different denominational viewpoints, you can still become the counselor of choice.

Many cities have trans-denominational ministerial associations. Find these groups and offer to be a guest speaker. Ask if notices of your groups or seminars can be given to ministers at each meeting or placed in the association bulletin. Some ministerial associations grant membership to allied professionals, such as counselors. Joining such a group is an excellent way to meet pastors from many different churches and denominations.

If your expertise and your calling are to serve a specific population, then you want to contact the appropriate pastor in charge of that group within each nearby church. Define your population as closely as possible to typical Sunday school classes and affinity groups in the church such as college students, single adults, young marrieds, or senior adults. Those are only a few examples. Fortunately, in the body of Christ all ages and stages of life are represented. Besides letting the pastor know of your counseling services, give information about weekend retreats, seminars, and other special programs you can provide for the special population.

Look for support groups and fellowships that reach out into the community. Some that are active in my area are Christian Business Owners, Women's Aglow, Nurses for Christ, and Fellowship of Christian Athletes. There are many more. As these believers meet together to share, pray, and study the application of biblical principles in their life situation, group leaders become aware of individuals with serious problems that need professional attention. Present yourself as a speaker and community resource person for the group. If you have the time and genuine interest, join the group. In either case, ask permission to distribute your brochures and group schedules to members or have these materials available at the registration table.

There are plenty of people who need counseling. Your task is to inform them both directly and indirectly (through referral sources) of the services you provide. Realize that your referral prospecting must be targeted. Begin with one or two of the groups most likely to be interested or those with whom you have an existing, positive rapport, then gradually add another affinity group to your prospecting efforts. Do not expect to cover all these potential sources; it is too time-consuming and not necessary. Instead separate the wheat from the chaff. Periodically revise, add, and eliminate until you find the referral sources that are most productive for you. Even after your schedule is full, never neglect referral prospecting. Although you can afford to devote less time to making new contacts, do not let your efforts or skills go stale. Your best referral source may move out of state, retire, or die. Successful counseling practices must never become too dependent upon current referrals or too complacent with today's full schedule. "Do not boast about tomorrow, for you do not know what a day may bring forth" (Prov. 27:1).

Epilogue

Working the PLAN

A prudent man foresees the difficulties ahead and prepares for them;
the simpleton goes blindly on and suffers the consequences.

Proverbs 22:3 TLB

As you read these closing comments, think ahead about the future of your counseling business. Let us say that you have survived the start-up year, you have kept within budget, and have experienced slow but steady growth in the numbers of new and referral clients. Perhaps this seems like the time to prop up your feet and relax, right? Wrong! According to the Small Business Administration, slightly more than half of all new businesses fail within the initial five years after start-up. You are not out of the woods yet. However, surviving the first year is significant and indicates a positive momentum. Now, let us look at how to turn surviving into thriving. As you work your PLAN consider these means of analyzing your ongoing operations.

P oint of diminishing returns
L ead by competence
A dhere to biblical foundations
N eutralize ambivalence

1. The point of diminishing returns is a measure of productivity that determines if expansion will improve profitability or reduce efficiency. In simple terms, more is not always better—it is just more. There is a real *point* at which more of a variable factor applied to a fixed factor fails to yield proportional results. For example, two counselors working a full-day schedule may see fourteen to sixteen clients. Adding a third counselor (the variable factor) may not proportionately increase the number of clients seen due to space restrictions or the need for supervision (fixed factors). Thus, productivity does not increase proportionately and may even decrease at the point of diminishing returns.

As you consider increasing the number of counselors or groups and expanding into larger office space, carefully weigh the real bottom-line impact of these changes. If your office is busy now and the waiting list of clients is growing, check your Practice Utilization Reviews (see Appendix K) to determine if this is a seasonal phenomenon or a consistently increasing need over the last six to nine months. Or have you been bitten by the *expansion bug?* Symptoms are: an irrational belief that early success is certain to continue; a personal desire to move ahead without money or adequate planning and then challenge God to fulfill your wish list; or misdirected ambition that craves the adrenaline high of launching new projects. "All man's efforts are for his mouth, yet his appetite is never satisfied. . . . Better what the eye sees than the roving of the appetite" (Eccles. 6:7, 9).

Expansion is not the predestined course of every small business. You can have a very successful counseling program by choosing to maintain a managed overhead and a small staff and by working with a closely defined target market or providing specialized services. Applying measures of efficiency and regular practice utilization reviews are still important to the business that chooses to remain small—there is less room for mistakes to be offset by volume.

2. The way to bring glory to the Lord and sustain a successful counseling business is to **lead by competence.** Christian counselors must set the standard for the highest level of services in the community. To do so, become a lifelong learner

who approaches continuing education with enthusiasm. Recognize the need to improve your skills, share ideas with other Christian counselors, and be willing to teach or mentor others. "Let the wise listen and add to their learning and let the discerning get guidance. . . . The fear of the LORD is the beginning of knowledge, but fools despise wisdom and discipline" (Prov. 1:5, 7). To present yourself to the public as a Christian counselor is to declare that you are personally related to Jesus. Make your work worthy of Him who called you to serve.

3. In all things, personal and professional, **adhere to Biblical foundations.** The essential principles of competent counseling appeared in Scripture hundreds of years before the writers of psychological theories were born. Know the God-inspired scriptural approaches to counseling so that you are not deceived by man-made versions. "All Scripture is God-breathed and is useful for teaching, rebuking, correcting and training in righteousness, so that the man of God may be thoroughly equipped for every good work" (2 Tim. 3:16). Also, learn the scriptural principles for business operations. You do not need an MBA to comprehend the practical yet profound advice about business management that is found in the Bible.

4. Be prepared to recognize and **neutralize ambivalence.** This paralyzing feeling can sneak up on you in two ways. The most obvious way is when financial pressures and personal problems overwhelm you so completely that victory seems out of reach. At that point it is easy to shrug your shoulders and claim you didn't really care anyway or to begin an unspoken campaign of neglect toward your faltering business. That "who cares?" attitude is more a faith problem than a business problem. Your business may not succeed in its present form, however, if you are busy masking your disappointment with ambivalence, and you will not have time or energy to pray for and receive the real answer.

Ambivalence can also occur when success is rapid and sustained. During the meteoric rise of your business, there simply was not enough time to decompress from the intensity of the start-up phase. Suddenly, you look around the office and see the staff operating at high efficiency, the profit and loss statements reflecting positive growth, and your business plan working smoothly. You feel proud—and restless and obsolete. Some people mistakenly think this is the time to change an already workable structure or leave it behind to start a new venture. Neither of these options offers long-term satisfaction nor business success.

Perhaps God has brought your counseling business to this stage because He has something new for you to learn or He wants you to make a renewed commitment to this enterprise. "The steps of a good man are ordered by the LORD" (Ps. 37:23 NKJV). Turn ambivalence into adventure by seeking the will of God and being open to accept His direction wherever it leads.

Let us finish with this final thought: As you work your PLAN have confidence in the promise that "we know that in all things God works for the good of those who love him, who have been called according to his purpose. . . . If God is for us, who can be against us?" (Rom. 8:28, 31).

Appendix A

Free Tax Services for Your Business

The Internal Revenue Service provides a variety of free services. Toll-free hotlines are answered Monday through Friday from 8 A.M. to 4:30 P.M. eastern time.

For questions about your tax return, call 1-800-829-1040.

To order free brochures or tax forms, call 1-800-829-3676.

Choose the brochures applicable to your business structure.

Publication number	Title
334	*Tax Guide for Small Business*
517	*Social Security for Members of the Clergy and Religious Workers*
533	*Self-Employment Tax*
534	*Depreciation*
535	*Business Expenses*
538	*Accounting Periods and Methods*
541	*Tax Information on Partnerships*
542	*Tax Information on Corporations*
551	*Basis of Assets*
557	*Tax-Exempt Status for Your Organization*
560	*Retirement Plans for the Self-Employed*
583	*Taxpayers Starting a Business*
589	*Tax Information on S Corporations*
598	*Tax on Unrelated Business Income of Exempt Organizations*
910	*Guide to Free Tax Services*
937	*Business Reporting*

Appendix B

Recommended Resources for the New Counseling Office

Diagnostic and Statistical Manual of Mental Disorders, 3d ed., revised (DSM-III-R), American Psychiatric Association, Washington, D.C., 1987.

1992 Guidebook to Fair Employment Practices (includes new requirements of Americans with Disabilities Act), $20. Commerce Clearing House, 4025 West Peterson Avenue, Chicago, Illinois 60646.

Psychotherapy Finances: Managing Your Practice and Your Money, monthly newsletter, $68 per year. Ridgewood Financial Institute, Inc., 1016 Clemons St., #407, Jupiter, Florida 33477. For more information call: 800-869-8450.

1993 U.S. Master Tax Guide, updated annually, $28.50. Commerce Clearing House, 4025 West Peterson Avenue, Chicago, Illinois 60646

Forms for Business, standard edition, $14.95. Visual Organizers Inc., Wood Dale, Illinois 1985. Contains 248 forms including financial, accounting, and operations, as well as graphic aids.

The Small Business Handbook, $18, by Irving Burstiner. Simon and Schuster: New York, 1989.

Cover Letters That Knock 'Em Dead by Martin Yate, $7.95. Bob Adams, Inc., Holbrook, Massachusetts, 1992. A collection of letters for business reply, networking, and follow-up. "Power phrases" are noted.

Webster's New World Secretarial Handbook, $12. Prentice Hall, New York, 1989. An updated guide to business letter and report formats, grammar, titles, and general office information.

Appendix C

Business Information Sources

U.S. Small Business Administration: A federal agency with regional offices to give technical assistance, management consultation and training for small business owners. Call the SBA hotline, 800-827-5722, or check your local directory for an SBA office in your area.

Small Business Development Center: These regional and local programs offer short courses and conferences on a variety of business development and management topics. Look for listings in your local directory or call the nearest SBA office.

SCORE/ACE: Members of the Service Corps of Retired Executives and the Active Corps of Executives are experienced business men and women who mentor new business owners. Check for listings in your local directory or call the nearest Small Business Development Center to contact SCORE/ACE.

U.S. Chamber of Commerce: This agency provides general business information. Contact the chamber at 1615 H. Street NW, Washington, D.C. 20062. Telephone 800-638-6582. Also contact the Small Business Center at the U.S. Chamber, 202-463-5503, to request a catalog of small business publications.

Mancuso's Small Business Resource Guide: This book by J. R. Mancuso gives names, addresses, and phone numbers of business information sources including advertising, public relations, banks, computer, marketing, legal services, and newsletters. Published by Prentice Hall, New York, 1988.

How to Write a Business Plan: This workbook by Mike McKeever has many useful forms, including cash flow, balance sheet, and profit and loss statement. Nolo Press, Berkeley, California, 1992.

National Association for the Self-Employed: A trade organization of independent business owners with buyers' benefits including insurance for self-employed and small businesses. Write to 2121 Precinct Line Road, Hurst, Texas 76054. Telephone 817-656-6313.

Small Business Reporter: Publishes booklets on various business topics for business owners and managers. Available from Bank of America, Dept. 3120, P.O. Box 37000, San Francisco, California 94137. Telephone 415-622-2491. $3 per copy. Write for a list of topics.

Consumer Information Catalog: Two hundred free and low-cost booklets on business management, personal finance, and other consumer topics. Consumer Information Center, Pueblo, Colorado 81009. Call 719-948-4000 to get on the mailing list for this quarterly catalog.

Appendix D

Computer Software for Counselors

Address and Phone Book: Coordinates with Day-Timer systems to sort, search, produce labels and rotary cards, and import or export data. $49.95 for IBM-compatibles; $79.95 for Macintosh. Day-Timers, Inc., One Day-Timer Plaza, Allentown, Pennsylvania 18195-1551. Telephone 215-266-9505.

Business Plan Toolkit: Templates for financial data, cash flow, balance sheet, and projected income forms plus narratives to create a complete business plan. Companion programs include; Marketing Plan Toolkit, Employee Plan Toolkit, and Business Budgeting Toolkit, all from Palo Alto Software. $149.95 each. Telphone: 800-336-5544.

Financial Management Techniques for Small Businesses: A choice of basic or more detailed versions of worksheets for business management. $69 to $129. Oasis Press, 300 N. Valley Drive, Grants Pass, Oregon 97526. Telephone 800-228-2275.

Print Your Page: Works with popular programs such as Lotus and WordPerfect to shrink or turn your workpages into Day-Timer size inserts for your personal or desk calendars. New in July 1993. Estimated price, $34.95. Day-Timers, Inc., One Day-Timer Plaza, Allentown, Pennsylvania 18195-1551. Telephone 215-266-9505.

Shrinkrapt: Billing and insurance set to print on new HCFA 1500 forms. Available in three versions: Solo Practitioner, $585, Multi-Practitioner, $985; and HCFC Form Filer (for low volume), $99. Saner Software, Inc., 37 W. 222 Rt. 64, Suite 253, St. Charles, Illinois 60175. Telephone 800-448-6899.

Successful Business Plans: Provides elements of business plans to adapt to your business. $69.95 software only. $89.95 software plus manual. Oasis Press, 300 N. Valley Dr., Grants Pass, Oregon 97526. Telephone 800-228-2275

Appendix E

Sample Press Release

I. M. Able, PhD, LPC
Able Counseling Center
1234 Busy Street
All America City, America 12345

FOR IMMEDIATE RELEASE

All American City, June 1—Able Counseling Center is sponsoring a training program for parents, counselors and child-care workers on "Finding Comfort in Play" from 9 A.M. to 3 P.M. Friday and Saturday, July 17 and 18, at Library Auditorium. This innovative program teaches adults how to use simplified techniques of play therapy to help children cope with loss, frustration, anger, and illness.

Dr. I. M. Able, director of Able Counseling Center, defines his program as "a healing journey for adults and the children in their care." Underscoring the value of this training, Pastor Ever Faithful said, "I can see a difference in the way our children's ministry workers relate to the preschoolers after completing the Able program."

Advance registration is required due to limited space. The fee is $30 per couple for parents and $25 each for counselors, teachers, ministry workers, and child-care workers. Call 123-4567 for registration information.

Note that the essential elements (who, what, when, where, and why) appear in the first brief paragraph. **Who:** Able Counseling Center. **What:** "Finding Comfort in Play." **When:** 9 A.M. to 3 P.M. Friday and Saturday, July 17 and 18. **Where:** Library Auditorium. **Why:** Teaches parents, counselors, and child-care workers how to use simplified concepts of play therapy to help children cope with loss, frustration, anger, and illness.

Two or three comments must be very quotable or catchy and made by people who are well known locally or nationally.

Type the press release double-spaced with wide margins. Check spelling and grammar. Get approval for quotes. Include a brochure of the event to give more background or spark interest for an interview.

Appendix F

Planning Marketing Contacts

Complete one page for every primary and secondary target client group and referral sources.

Target audience _____

Demographics: __male __female __18–35 __35–49 __49–60 __60+
__high school education __college education __professional/graduate education
__Caucasian __African-American __Hispanic __Asian __American Indian __other:
__single adults __two-parent families __single-parent families __retirees
average income: __under $20,000 ___$20,000–$40,000 __$40,000–$60,000 __over $60,000

Geographic proximity of target audience to your office:_____

Objective of contact (check all that apply):

__introduction __good will __seek referrals __promote workshop __recommend action
__consultation __schedule speech or workshop __offer newsletter __reinforce loyalty

Communication channels to use (rank by priority all that apply)

__personal visit __telephone __letter __fax __church workshop __community workshop
__speech at public location __speech to civic, social, or church group __newsletter
__major newspaper advertisement __community newspaper advertisement __bulletin notice
__radio spot announcements __radio public service announcements __cable TV commercials
__radio interview show __TV interview show __cable TV interview
__other ideas:

What materials do you need for this contact?

__business cards __general brochure __special event brochure __workshop schedule

Describe the message you want to communicate in fifty words or less:

_____

_____

How will you measure the success of this contact? __no. of new appointments
__no. who attend workshop__no. of new information requests __no. of new referrals
Other:

Appendix G

Balance Sheet

Date, 19___

CURRENT ASSETS

Cash $ _____
Accounts receivable   _____
Inventory (i.e., therapeutic products, brochures)   _____

FIXED ASSETS

Real Estate   _____
Equipment   _____
Vehicles   _____

         TOTAL ASSETS   _____

CURRENT LIABILITIES

Accounts payable $ _____
Accrued expenses   _____
Loans payable (within one year)   _____

LONG-TERM LIABILITIES

Loans payable (longer than one year)   _____

         TOTAL LIABILITIES   _____

NET WORTH (TOTAL ASSETS minus TOTAL LIABILITIES)   _____

Note: This is a very basic format. Add more specific categories of assets and liabilities as needed for a more complete financial picture of your business.

Appendix H

Income Statement

for Month Ended 19___

INCOME

Counseling fees

Insurance reimbursement

Consultation or supervision

Testing and evaluations

Workshops

Printed products

Rent from associates

Other:

TOTAL (GROSS) INCOME

EXPENSES

Advertising and marketing

Continuing education

Dues and publications

Insurance

Licenses

Loan payments

Office supplies

Postage

Printing and stationery

Rent for office

Rent for vehicles or equipment

Repairs and maintenance

Salaries

Taxes on payroll

Taxes on income (federal, state, local)

Telephone and other communications

Tithe

Transportation

Utilities

Other:

TOTAL EXPENSES

NET INCOME (LOSS)*

* Total Income minus Total Expenses = Net Income [if positive] or Net Loss [if negative]

Appendix I

Guidelines for Selecting an Office Location

Place an X by each amenity that is necessary and an O by each optional amenity. Bring a copy of this page with you when viewing potential offices. Use a separate page for each office visited. Rate the amenities as: 1=excellent, 2=good, 3=adequate, 4=not adequate

Address:_____

Describe: __direct entry/ground floor __two- to three-story building __high-rise __converted house
__office park __medical building __office condos __separate building

Minimum size needed: ____sq. ft. per counseling office ___sq. ft. reception / secretarial
Total number counseling offices needed ___ Group room ____sq. ft.

Amenities	Requirements	Rating	Comments
Parking			
Elevator (second floor and above)			
Handicapped access			
Entry direct to hall or outside			
Shared reception area			
Pays own utilities			
Utilities provided			
Controls own AC/heat unit			
Building controls AC/heat			
Cleaning service provided			
Sign: Your name on marquee			
Sign: Your name on door			

(Continues on next page)

Easy-to-find location
Near public transportation
Other counselors in building
Other professionals in building
Mixed-use offices in building
Good lighting at night
Building security
Extent of soundproofing in walls
Carpeting: quality and color
Bathroom: private or public
Private entrance for counselor
Allows tenant to paint or change decor
Expansion potential

Appendix J

Counseling Fee Analysis

Follow this example to determine how many clients at what fee you must serve in order to meet office expenses and pay your salary. Use the estimated total expenses from your start-up budget or income statement.

Determine your total number of work days per year. This example uses: 260 potential workdays minus 7 holidays minus 8 vacation or sick days = 245 workdays

Salary you desire: $40,000   (gross salary, before taxes)
Total annual operating expenses: $10,000

Total expenses divided by work days = Daily operating costs
   $10,000   divided by   245   = $40.82

Annual salary   divided by work days = Daily salary allocation
   $40,000   divided by   245   = $163.26

Daily operating costs + daily salary allocation = required daily earnings
   $40.82   + $163.26   = $204.08

If you have not determined a session fee or are considering changing fees, calculate several fee amounts to discover how many paid sessions are needed to cover required daily earnings.

Required Daily Earnings divided by Per Session Fee = Minimum Daily Paid Sessions

$204.08	divided by	$40	=	5	sessions
$204.08	divided by	$50	=	4	sessions
$204.08	divided by	$60	=	3.5	sessions
$204.08	divided by	$70	=	3	sessions
$204.08	divided by	$80	=	2.5	sessions

Appendix K

Practice Utilization Review

Direct Client Services	Monthly Total	Quarterly Total	Year to Date Total
Intakes with new clients			
Intakes with referral clients			
Individual sessions			
EAP referrals			
PPO referrals			
Testing and evaluations			
Marriage counseling			
Consultation sessions			
Supervision sessions			

Services to groups	number in group	groups monthly	groups quarterly	groups, year to date
Therapy groups				
Growth groups				
Educational groups				
Workshops				

Analysis of Services

	Current monthly total	Same month prior year	Change + or -	Ratio of Change as percentage
Direct client services	_____	_____	_____	_____
Services to groups	_____	_____	_____	_____

(Continues on next page)

Key Questions to Answer

1. What are the two most productive services?

2. What are the reasons for their success? (i.e., marketing, referrals, workshops, etc.)

3. What are the two least productive services?

4. What are the reasons for low productivity? (i.e., lack of marketing, ineffective marketing, failure to meet needs of target market, price, etc.)

Appendix L

Workshop or Seminar Planning Guide

Program title _____

Date _____ Time _____ Place _____ Estimated audience _____

Speaker(s) _____ Assistant(s) _____

Primary Goal _____

Secondary Goal _____

date   assigned to   done

Confirmations given or received

Research or writing for program

Order printing, brochures, etc.

Prepare advertising campaign

Purchase ad space; review ad copy

Establish preregistration procedures

Issue press release

Contract for sound system or equipment

Arrange for food or beverage service

Order supplies (i.e. nametags, pencils, etc.)

Prepare audio-visual materials

Make on-site inspection (day before program)

Arrive early for set-up

Remove equipment after program

Day after program: audit results and note
things you can do better in future programs.

Appendix M

Crisis Prevention Tips for Your Workshop

View the room several weeks before the seminar. Check for:

_____Electric outlets for audio-visual equipment.

_____Podium or table for speaker's notes.

_____Quality of sound system.

_____Arrangement of seats (fixed or flexible).

_____A table outside the room for registration and product displays.

_____Easy access for handicapped persons.

_____Proximity of rest rooms.

_____Approval to place signs outside meeting room door.

_____Confirm what groups are meeting near your room at the same time.

Audio-visual equipment:

_____Know how to set up all the equipment you bring (you may not always get help).

_____Get a 25 ft. remote control cord for the slide projector.

_____Bring spare parts: extra bulb for projector, extra batteries for recorder, power cords.

_____Have a good-quality copy of your audio or video tape in case the original breaks.

_____Use your own projector that you know how to use.

Printed materials:

_____Have five extra workbooks or packets for every fifteen estimated attendees.

_____Display your practice brochures at the registration table and in the meeting room.

_____Give attendees a schedule of any programs you will be presenting during the next three to six months.

_____Arrange to sell copies of your books, tapes, or other therapeutic products.

_____Bring a master copy of your outline so extras can be made on site if the crowd is very large.

_____Preprint name tags if attendees preregister.

Facility services:

_____Ask who is responsible for room arrangement and other setups.

_____Get the name of the maintenance crew leader on duty during your workshop.

_____If no managers are on duty during your meeting, get their emergency or pager number.

_____Introduce yourself to the front desk or reception personnel when you arrive.

Outdoor events:

_____Consider a tent or alternative site in the event of foul weather.

_____Rent an adequate sound system and hire an experienced sound technician to run it.

_____Ask the city and county if any permits are needed for the outdoor assembly.

_____If food is served, hire a caterer or get proper food service permits (city or county).

_____Hire a police officer to direct traffic if you expect a large number of cars.

Appendix N

New-Client Forms

PERSONAL AND FAMILY RECORD

To make our first meeting more productive, please give accurate and complete responses to every section of this form. If necessary, write additional information in the margins.

Date_____
Client Name _____ Age ___ Birthdate _____
Address _____ City _____ State ___ Zip _____
Phone (home) _____ (work) _____ best times to call _____
Employed by _____ How long? _____ Position _____
Social security number _____ Previous type of work _____

Circle last year of school completed: 9 10 11 12 GED College: 1 2 3 4
Other_____
Marital status:
single, never married___ engaged___ living together without marriage___
separated__ how long?__ divorced__ how long?__ widow/er __ how long?__
Married__ Spouse name_____ Age____ Occupation_____
How long married to this spouse?_____ Are you happy in this marriage?_____
Total number prior marriages for you_____ For your spouse _____

Children	Age	Sex	Relationship to You?	Live in your home?
_____			_____	_____
_____	__	__	_____	_____
_____	__	__	_____	_____
_____	__	__	_____	_____

COUNSELING HISTORY

Have you ever been to Counseling for any reason? Yes___No ___
What reason? _____ How long? ____Counselor _____

224

Are you presently working with any other Counselor or Psychologist? Yes__ No__
What reason? _____How long? ____Counselor _____

Are you involved in any other marriage counseling, family counseling, or support groups? Yes__ No__ Specify _____

Briefly state the nature of the problem as you see it: _____
_____

What do you want to gain from counseling? _____

Who referred you to this counseling office? _____

What is your religious preference? _____Church _____
How strong is the influence of your church in your life? _____
Pastor _____

MEDICAL INFORMATION

Family Physician_____Psychiarist/Psychologist _____
Are you taking any prescription drugs? Yes___ No___ If yes, state the drug name(s), type, and for what purpose: _____
Who prescribed the drug(s)? _____
How often do you see this doctor? _____
Describe your physical health: excellent___ good___ adequate___ poor___
Are you taking prescription drugs for emotional distress? Yes __No___If yes, state the drug name(s): _____
Who prescribed the drug(s)? _____How often do you see this doctor? ___
Have you ever been hospitalized for mental illness or substance abuse? Yes ____No ____ If yes, for what reason? _____
How long were you in treatment? _____
Hospital name _____How long ago? _____
Did you continue with outpatient counseling? Yes__ No__
Name of counselor _____

IMPACT OF LIFE CIRCUMSTANCES

Circle any LOSSES that you have experienced:
Death of: spouse, child, father, mother, sister, brother, grandmother, grandfather, friend. Divorce Separation Broken engagement Suicide Miscarriage Abortion Infertility Bankruptcy Homelessness Career or job loss Other:_____

Circle any VICTIMIZATIONS you have experienced or been involved with:
Child abuse: physical, emotional, sexual, incest
Spouse abuse: physical, emotional, sexual
Abandonment   Rape   Robbery   Assault   Suicide attempt   Auto or industrial accident
Major illness   Surgery   Physical disability   Alienation, Other: _____

Circle any PROBLEMS that concern you now:
Relationship(s) with: Spouse   Children   Parents   In-laws   Co-workers   Friends   Teachers
Alcohol   Street Drugs   Prescription drugs   Binge eating   Excessive dieting or exercise
Shopping   Work too much   Procrastination   Communication   Depression   Anger   Grief
Gender identity   Sex   Career   Loneliness   Mood swings   Self-esteem   Codependency   Stress   Fear   Anxiety   Feelings about church or God   Other_____

INTENSE EMOTIONAL DISTRESS

<u>Current Situation</u>   <u>Explanation</u>
Suicidal thoughts, plans, attempts _____
Homicidal thoughts, plans, attempts _____
Desire to cause pain to self or others _____
In fear for your life or personal safety _____
Too depressed to care for self or family _____

In signing below, I affirm that the information given on this form is true and complete.

_____ Date _____ For minor: _____
Client or Custodial Parent or Guardian

CONSENT FOR RELEASE OF INFORMATION

Counselor name
Name of Counseling Center
License number or certifications
Address
City   State   Zip   Phone

I, _____ date of birth _____, do consent and authorize the following by writing YES or No by each section and completing all applicable blanks:

_____any Attorney, Agency, Mental Health Center, Case Manager, Counseling Center, School System, Medical Facility, Physician, Psychologist, Psychotherapist, Pastoral Counselor or other Counselor to provide the above named Counselor any information about me concerning any illness, injury, medical history, consultation, prescriptions, treatment plans, progress reports, testing and appraisals or other information from medical, social service, or consultation records.

_____communicate by telephone or in writing with my Physician, Case Manager, Attorney or Attorney's representative as needed to assist the other professional in working with me.
Name of professional _____ Phone _____
Address _____ City _____ State ___ Zip _____

_____release all of my counseling records to: Counselor _____
Address _____ City _____ State ___ Zip _____
Office Phone _____

_____release my counseling records with the exeception of _____
To: Counselor _____ Address _____
City _____ State ___ Zip _____ Office Phone _____

A photostatic copy of this authorization shall be considered as effective and valid as the original. At anytime, I may make written request to withdraw this release of information. Such withdrawal must be presented to the therapist to whom this consent was originally given.

_____ _____ _____
Signature of Client or Guardian   Date signed   Social security number

Name of minor client or adult client under guardianship is _____
If Guardian, legal authority is as: Parent___ Custodial parent____ Trustee ____
Court-appointed guardian___ If other, specify:_____

FINANCIAL ASSIGNMENT AND RELEASE

Counselor name
Name of Counseling Center
License number or certifications
Address
City   State   Zip   Phone

I agree to pay the above named provider for all psychotherapy services rendered and attest that I have been informed of said charges.

If psychotherapy services are covered by private insurance, benefits due to me under existing policies are hereby assigned to the above named provider. I permit a copy of the signature on this release to serve as a lifetime authorization. A copy of this form may be used in place of the original. This provider does not offer services under Medicare or Medicaid.

I understand that specific diagnostic and treatment information may be required by third party payors and I consent to release of all requested information.

I understand that I (or the person signed as financially responsible) am personally responsibile for the costs of psychotherapy services including but not limited to; unmet deductible, co-payment and any fees or portions of fees not paid by my insurance carrier.

Payment for services is expected at the time services are rendered. Failure to keep payments current or to arrange and maintain a payment plan for services not covered by insurance will result in collection action for the balance due.

The fee is: $____per 50 minute sesson or $ ____per 30 minute session
$____per group for ___weeks $ ____testing and evaluation

I hereby consent to treatment and affirm that this financial assignment and release has been explained to me. I agree to abide by these terms.

Client _____ Birthdate _____ SSN _____
Signature of responsible party if other than Client _____

Insurance Co. _____ Phone _____
Address _____ City _____ State ___ Zip _____
Policy # _____ Group # _____ Mental health outpatient limits _____

Appendix O

Professional and Pastoral Counseling Organizations

American Association for Marriage and Family Therapy   202-452-0109
1100 Seventeenth Street NW, Tenth Floor, Washington, D.C. 20036-4601

American Counseling Association   800-347-6647
5999 Stevenson Avenue, Alexandria, Virginia 22304-3300

American Association of Christian Counselors   800-5-COUNSEL
2421 West Pratt Avenue, Suite 1398, Chicago, Illinois 60645

American Association of Pastoral Counselors   703-385-6967
9504-A Lee Highway, Fairfax, Virginia 22031-2303

American Psychological Association   202-336-5500
750 First Streeet NE, Washington, D.C. 20002

Christian Association for Psychological Studies   909-695-CAPS
P.O. Box 890279, Temecula, California 92589-0279

National Association of Social Workers   800-638-8799
750 First Street NE, Suite 700, Washington, D.C. 20002-4241

National Board for Certified Counselors   800-398-5389
3-D Terrace Way, Greensboro, North Carolina 27403

Christian Business and Ministry Organizations

Christian Management Association   909-861-8861
P.O. Box 4683, Diamond Bar, California 91765
(conferences, regional chapters, books, and training institutes for certification in fund-raising, financial management, marketing, information management, human resources, and church management)

Christian Stewardship Association   708-690-0016
P.O. Box 8, Wheaton, Illinois 60189-0008
(conferences, newsletter, print resources, and networking directory)

Evangelical Council for Financial Accountability   800-323-9473
(excellent books and reporting guidelines for nonprofit organizations)

Bibliography

Abromovitz, Les. *Family Insurance Handbook: A Complete Guide for the 1990s.* Blue Ridge Summit, Pa.: Liberty Hall Press, 1990.

Adams, Robert L. *Ten-Second Business Forms.* Holbrook, Mass.: Bob Adams Publishing, 1987.

Adler, Elizabeth. *Print That Works.* Palo Alto, Calif.: Bull Publishing Co., 1991.

Bliss, Edwin. *Doing It Now: A Twelve-Step Program for Curing Procrastination and Achieving Your Goals.* New York: Bantam Books, 1984.

Brock, Susan, and Cabbell, Sally. *Writing a Human Resources Manual.* Ontario, Canada: Reid Publishing, 1989.

Clemente, Mark, ed. *The Marketing Glossary.* New York: AMACOM, 1992.

Cutlip, Scott, and Center, Allen. *Effective Public Relations*, 4th ed. Englewood Cliffs, N.J.: Prentice Hall, 1971.

Edwards, Sarah and Paul Edwards. *Making It On Your Own: Surviving and Thriving on the Ups and Downs of Being Your Own Boss*. Los Angeles: Jeremy P. Tarcher, 1991.

Fallon, William, ed. *AMA Management Handbook*, 2d ed. New York: AMACOM, 1983.

Goff, Christine Friesleben. *The Publicity Process*. 3d ed. Ames, Iowa: Iowa State University Press, 1989.

Goldstein, H. A. *122 Minutes a Month to Greater Profits*. Los Angeles: Granville Publishing, 1985.

Gumpert, D. E. *How to Really Create A Successful Business Plan*. Boston: Inc. Publishing, 1990.

LeBoeuf, Michael. *Working Smart*. New York: Warner Books, 1979.

Levicoff, Steve. "The Final Word," *Christian Counseling Today*, American Association of Christian Counselors, 1993

Marder, Joyce S., *Surviving the Start-Up Years In Your Own Business*. Whitehall, W. Va.: Betterway Publications, 1991.

Maydew, Gary L. *Small Business Taxation: Planning and Practice*. Chicago: Commerce Clearing House, 1992.

McKeever, Mike. *How to Write a Business Plan*. Berkeley, Calif.: Nolo Press, 1992.

Nadar, Ralph, and Smith, Wesley. *Winning the Insurance Game*. New York: Knightbridge Publishing, 1990.

Ohlschlager, George, and Mosgofian, Peter. *Law for the Christian Counselor*. Dallas: Word, 1992.

1993 U.S. Master Tax Guide. Chicago: Commerce Clearing House, 1992.

Psychotherapy Finances (newsletter), vol. 19, no. 3, and vol. 17, no. 12. Jupiter, Fla.: Ridgewood Financial Institute.

Richards, Daniel L. *Building and Managing Your Private Practice.* Alexandria, Va: American Association for Counseling and Development, 1990.

Sweeny, H. W. Allen, and Rachlin, Robert eds. *Handbook of Budgeting.* New York: John Wiley and Sons, 1981.

Thomas, David, and Fryar, Maridell . *Successful Business Speaking.* Skokie, Ill.: National Textbook, 1981.

Winston, William J., *How to Write a Marketing Plan for Health Care Organizations.* New York: Haworth Press, 1985.

Index

About the Author

Dr. Kathie Tanner Erwin is a clinical psychotherapist in private practice in Florida. She has an M.A. in counseling psychology from Liberty University, and an M.B.A. and a Ph.D. in Human Resources Management from California Coast University. She is a National Certified Counselor, a National Certified Gerontological Counselor, a Licensed Mental Health Counselor, an Accredited Public Relations Professional (ADRP), and a Certified Financial Planner (CFP).

Dr. Erwin has enjoyed success in three interesting careers: radio and television news, financial planning, and psychotherapy. She is in high demand as a seminar speaker and teacher, and has been honored as Woman of the Year by the American Business Women's Association.